C-2320   **CAREER EXAMINATION SERIES**

*This is your
PASSBOOK for...*

Senior Social Welfare Examiner

*Test Preparation Study Guide
Questions & Answers*

COPYRIGHT NOTICE

This book is SOLELY intended for, is sold ONLY to, and its use is RESTRICTED to individual, bona fide applicants or candidates who qualify by virtue of having seriously filed applications for appropriate license, certificate, professional and/or promotional advancement, higher school matriculation, scholarship, or other legitimate requirements of education and/or governmental authorities.

This book is NOT intended for use, class instruction, tutoring, training, duplication, copying, reprinting, excerption, or adaptation, etc., by:

1) Other publishers
2) Proprietors and/or Instructors of "Coaching" and/or Preparatory Courses
3) Personnel and/or Training Divisions of commercial, industrial, and governmental organizations
4) Schools, colleges, or universities and/or their departments and staffs, including teachers and other personnel
5) Testing Agencies or Bureaus
6) Study groups which seek by the purchase of a single volume to copy and/or duplicate and/or adapt this material for use by the group as a whole without having purchased individual volumes for each of the members of the group
7) Et al.

Such persons would be in violation of appropriate Federal and State statutes.

PROVISION OF LICENSING AGREEMENTS – Recognized educational, commercial, industrial, and governmental institutions and organizations, and others legitimately engaged in educational pursuits, including training, testing, and measurement activities, may address request for a licensing agreement to the copyright owners, who will determine whether, and under what conditions, including fees and charges, the materials in this book may be used them. In other words, a licensing facility exists for the legitimate use of the material in this book on other than an individual basis. However, it is asseverated and affirmed here that the material in this book CANNOT be used without the receipt of the express permission of such a licensing agreement from the Publishers. Inquiries re licensing should be addressed to the company, attention rights and permissions department.

All rights reserved, including the right of reproduction in whole or in part, in any form or by any means, electronic or mechanical, including photocopying, recording, or by any information storage and retrieval system, without permission in writing from the Publisher.

Copyright © 2024 by
National Learning Corporation

212 Michael Drive, Syosset, NY 11791
(516) 921-8888 • www.passbooks.com
E-mail: info@passbooks.com

PASSBOOK® SERIES

THE *PASSBOOK® SERIES* has been created to prepare applicants and candidates for the ultimate academic battlefield – the examination room.

At some time in our lives, each and every one of us may be required to take an examination – for validation, matriculation, admission, qualification, registration, certification, or licensure.

Based on the assumption that every applicant or candidate has met the basic formal educational standards, has taken the required number of courses, and read the necessary texts, the *PASSBOOK® SERIES* furnishes the one special preparation which may assure passing with confidence, instead of failing with insecurity. Examination questions – together with answers – are furnished as the basic vehicle for study so that the mysteries of the examination and its compounding difficulties may be eliminated or diminished by a sure method.

This book is meant to help you pass your examination provided that you qualify and are serious in your objective.

The entire field is reviewed through the huge store of content information which is succinctly presented through a provocative and challenging approach – the question-and-answer method.

A climate of success is established by furnishing the correct answers at the end of each test.

You soon learn to recognize types of questions, forms of questions, and patterns of questioning. You may even begin to anticipate expected outcomes.

You perceive that many questions are repeated or adapted so that you can gain acute insights, which may enable you to score many sure points.

You learn how to confront new questions, or types of questions, and to attack them confidently and work out the correct answers.

You note objectives and emphases, and recognize pitfalls and dangers, so that you may make positive educational adjustments.

Moreover, you are kept fully informed in relation to new concepts, methods, practices, and directions in the field.

You discover that you are actually taking the examination all the time: you are preparing for the examination by "taking" an examination, not by reading extraneous and/or supererogatory textbooks.

In short, this PASSBOOK®, used directedly, should be an important factor in helping you to pass your test.

SENIOR SOCIAL WELFARE EXAMINER

DUTIES
Participates in and supervises the activities of a group of subordinate examiners; performs categorical eligibility functions; makes field visits for the purpose of certifying eligibility; performs related duties as required.

SUBJECT OF THE EXAMINATION
The multiple-choice written test will cover knowledge, skills and lor abilities in such areas as:
1. Interpreting and applying written Social Welfare program materials and using basic arithmetic in determining eligibility for assistance;
2. Interviewing;
3. Preparing written material; and
4. Supervision.

INTRODUCTION

This test guide provides a general description of the subject areas which will be tested and the different types of questions you may see on the tests for Social Welfare Examiner, Senior Social Welfare Examiner, and related titles.

Following is a list of the five subject areas included on the tests for these titles. The announcement(s) for the examination(s) you are taking will tell you the subject areas on which you will be tested. Some examinations may involve subject areas which are not included in this or any other test guide.

1. **INTERVIEWING:** You must apply principles and techniques of interviewing to such problems as asking and answering questions, explaining requirements and helping the client understand his or her responsibilities, helping the client feel at ease, structuring and controlling the interview, reacting appropriately to inconsistencies, dealing with a variety of feelings of clients, maintaining confidentiality, and identifying the need for and making appropriate referrals. In addition, some questions may deal with contacting or interacting with other community organizations and agencies to benefit the client or the general public.
2. **RECORDING CASE NOTES:** You will be given several sentences from a typical case report paragraph and one additional sentence. You must determine the best place in the paragraph to put the additional sentence in order to make the report coherent and meaningful.
3. **INTERPRETING AND APPLYING WRITTEN SOCIAL WELFARE PROGRAM MATERIALS, AND USING BASIC ARITHMETIC IN DETERMINING ELIGIBILITY FOR ASSISTANCE:** You will be presented with written passages related to Social Services policies and procedures and be asked to interpret their meaning and/or apply this material to hypothetical case situations. Secondly, you will be given sets of written instructions and regulations regarding such Social Services programs as cash assistance, medical assistance, and Supplemental Nutrition Assistance Program (SNAP) benefits. You must read and understand the instructions given, including schedules of arithmetic figures, and apply these instructions to hypothetical case problems. Some questions require using arithmetic to compute the correct amount of assistance. Previous knowledge of Social Services programs or the eligibility process is not required.
4. **PREPARING WRITTEN MATERIAL:** These questions test for the ability to present information clearly and accurately, and to organize paragraphs logically and comprehensibly. For some questions, you will be given information in two or three sentences followed by four restatements of the information. You must then choose the best version. For other questions, you will be given paragraphs with their sentences out of order. You must then choose, from four suggestions, the best order for the sentences.
5. **SUPERVISION:** These questions test for knowledge of the principles and practices employed in planning, organizing, and controlling the activities of a work unit toward predetermined objectives. The concepts covered, usually in a situational question format, include such topics as assigning and reviewing work; evaluating performance; maintaining work standards; motivating and developing subordinates; implementing procedural change; increasing efficiency; and dealing with problems of absenteeism, morale, and discipline.

The next sections of this test guide explain how you will be tested in each of the subject areas listed above. A **TEST TASK** is provided for each subject area. This is an explanation of how a question is presented and how to correctly answer it. Read each explanation carefully. This test guide also provides at least one **SAMPLE QUESTION** for each subject area. The sample question is similar to the type of questions that will be presented on the actual test. This test guide provides the **SOLUTION** and correct answer to each sample question. You should study each sample question and solution in order to understand how the correct answer was determined.

SUBJECT AREA 1

INTERVIEWING: You must apply principles and techniques of interviewing to such problems as asking and answering questions, explaining requirements and helping the client understand his or her responsibilities, helping the client feel at ease, structuring and controlling the interview, reacting appropriately to inconsistencies, dealing with a variety of feelings of clients, maintaining confidentiality, and identifying the need for and making appropriate referrals. In addition, some questions may deal with contacting or interacting with other community organizations and agencies to benefit the client or the general public.

TEST TASK: You will be presented with questions that describe specific client-worker situations. Each question will be followed by four choices listing different ways to handle the situation. You must select the most appropriate course of action to take, based on an analysis of the situation, the application of the information provided, and the ramifications of various interviewing principles and strategies. *Note: You may be able to think of a better approach than any of the choices provided, but you must pick the best of those provided.*

SAMPLE QUESTION:

You have been reviewing an application for public assistance with a client and are satisfied that you have all the information necessary to make an eligibility determination. However, the client just will not stop talking and is repeating, in slightly different words, the information that he has already given you. Which one of the following is the best way to deal with this situation?

   A. Tell the client that the interview time is up and that if he has more to say, you can set up another appointment for the near future.
   B. Thank the client for the information. Tell him that you believe you have all that you need and that you will contact him if you should need additional information.
   C. Tell the client you would like to hear more, but that it will have to be postponed to some future date.
   D. Thank the client for coming in, but explain that others are waiting so you must end the interview.

The correct answer to this sample question is B.

SOLUTION:

Choice A gives the initiative to schedule another appointment to the client. This may lead to an unnecessary appointment. You already have enough information to make the necessary decisions, and there is no need for another appointment with the client in the near future.

Choice B is the correct answer to this question. By thanking the client for the information, you are being positive. By telling him that you believe you have what you need, you continue in this positive direction. By telling him that you will contact him if you need additional information, you make it clear that you have the necessary data, and you maintain the initiative to schedule another appointment.

Choice C, like choice A, gives the initiative to schedule another appointment to the client and may result in an unnecessary appointment. Also, telling the client you would like to hear more, but postponing it to some future date, is contradictory and sends the client a mixed message.

Choice D begins well -- thanking the client for coming in is positive. However, explaining that others are waiting so you must end the interview leaves the client with the impression that you are rushing him out and that you are more concerned with the people who are waiting than you are with him.

SUBJECT AREA 2

RECORDING CASE NOTES: You will be given several sentences from a typical case report paragraph and one additional sentence. You must determine the best place in the paragraph to put the additional sentence in order to make the report coherent and meaningful.

TEST TASK: You will be presented with a number of sentences which should be read **in order**, to make up **most** of a well-organized paragraph. Below them appears a single sentence, labeled X, which has its proper place at the beginning, in the body, or at the end of the paragraph. You must decide which of the four choices, A, B, C, or D, describes the **best** location for Sentence X.

SAMPLE QUESTION:

1. A fire has destroyed the apartment in which a client's family was residing.
2. The family was placed in emergency housing for one evening.
3. The rent and utility connection bills were paid by emergency grant.
4. The children were registered in their new school district.
5. The family was given funds for the purchase of new furniture.

In which position does **Sentence X** best fit the above paragraph?

Sentence X – The next day, the family found an apartment for the same rent they had been paying.

A. before sentence 1
B. between sentences 2 and 3
C. between sentences 3 and 4
D. between sentences 4 and 5

The correct answer to this sample question is B.

SOLUTION:

Choice A *would present the information out of sequence. The first sentence should introduce the subject that the case record is about. This choice starts the paragraph with "The next day" which clearly indicates that something else happened first. So Sentence X cannot begin the paragraph.*

Choice B is the correct answer to this question. *It presents the information in the paragraph in the best logical sequence. The family's immediate shelter need had to be addressed before they could search for another apartment.*

Choices C and D *also present the information out of sequence. The family would have to find a new apartment before they could arrange for the payment of rent and utility bills. They would also need to know the location of the new apartment in order to determine the appropriate school district in which to register the children.*

SUBJECT AREA 3

INTERPRETING AND APPLYING WRITTEN SOCIAL WELFARE PROGRAM MATERIALS, AND USING BASIC ARITHMETIC IN DETERMINING ELIGIBILITY FOR ASSISTANCE: You will be presented with written passages related to Social Services policies and procedures and be asked to interpret their meaning and/or apply this material to hypothetical case situations. Secondly, you will be given sets of written instructions and regulations regarding such Social Services programs as cash assistance, medical assistance, and Supplemental Nutrition Assistance Program (SNAP) benefits. You must read and understand the instructions given, including schedules of arithmetic figures, and apply these instructions to hypothetical case problems. Some questions require using arithmetic to compute the correct amount of assistance. Previous knowledge of Social Services programs or the eligibility process is not required.

TEST TASK: You will be given sets of written instructions and regulations regarding such Social Services programs as cash assistance, medical assistance, and food stamps. You must read and understand the instructions given, including schedules of arithmetic figures, and apply these instructions to hypothetical client situations.

NOTE: You will be allowed to bring a calculator and use it during the test.

SAMPLE QUESTION:

Single individuals and childless couples between 21 and 64 years of age and not blind or disabled are eligible for inpatient care and services under the catastrophic illness provision. Under this provision, the applicant is responsible for the cost of medical care equal to the lesser of (a) 25% of his annual net income, or (b) the amount of annual net income in excess of the cash assistance eligibility level.

Cash Assistance Eligibility Levels

Number in Household	1	2
Annual Cash Assistance Eligibility Level	$2,210	$3,180

Assuming that Mr. and Mrs. Jones, age 62 and 61 respectively, are otherwise eligible, which one of the following is the amount of their financial responsibility for inpatient care and services for Mrs. Jones if their annual net income is $3,400 and their hospital bill is $4,000?

A. $ 220
B. $ 850
C. $1,000
D. $1,190

The correct answer to this sample question is A.

SOLUTION:

*To arrive at the correct answer, you must calculate the figure obtained from both method (a) and method (b) and then use the lower figure obtained. Under (a) 25% of the annual net income is $850 (0.25 X $3,400). Under (b) the amount of annual net income in excess of the cash assistance eligibility level for **two** people is $220 ($3,400 - $3,180). Since $220 is the **lesser** of the two figures obtained, this is the amount of their financial responsibility for inpatient care and services for Mrs. Jones.* **(choice A)**

SUBJECT AREA 4

PREPARING WRITTEN MATERIAL:

These questions test for the ability to present information clearly and accurately, and to organize paragraphs logically and comprehensibly. For some questions, you will be given information in two or three sentences followed by four restatements of the information. You must then choose the best version. For other questions, you will be given paragraphs with their sentences out of order. You must then choose, from four suggestions, the best order for the sentences.

TEST TASK: There are two separate test tasks in this subject area.

- For the first, **Information Presentation**, you will be given information in two or three sentences, followed by four restatements of the information. You must then select the choice which presents the information most clearly, accurately, and completely.

- For the second, **Paragraph Organization**, you will be given paragraphs with their sentences out of order, and then be asked to choose, from among four suggestions, the best order for the sentences.

INFORMATION PRESENTATION SAMPLE QUESTION:

Martin Wilson failed to take proper precautions. His failure to take proper precautions caused a personal injury accident.

Which one of the following best presents the information above?

A. Martin Wilson failed to take proper precautions that caused a personal injury accident.
B. Proper precautions, which Martin Wilson failed to take, caused a personal injury accident.
C. Martin Wilson's failure to take proper precautions caused a personal injury accident.
D. Martin Wilson, who failed to take proper precautions, was in a personal injury accident.

The correct answer to this sample question is C.

SOLUTION:

Choice A conveys the incorrect impression that proper precautions caused a personal injury accident.

Choice B conveys the incorrect impression that proper precautions caused a personal injury accident.

Choice C is the correct answer to this question. *It best presents the original information: Martin Wilson failed to take proper precautions and this failure caused a personal injury accident.*

Choice D states that Martin Wilson was in a personal injury accident. The original information states that Martin Wilson caused a personal injury accident, but it does not state that Martin Wilson was in a personal injury accident.

SUBJECT AREA 4 (cont.)

PREPARING WRITTEN MATERIAL (cont.)

PARAGRAPH ORGANIZATION SAMPLE QUESTION:

The following question is based upon a group of sentences. The sentences are shown out of sequence, but when correctly arranged, they form a connected, well-organized paragraph. Read the sentences, and then answer the question about the best arrangement of these sentences.

1. Eventually, they piece all of this information together and make a choice.

2. Before actually deciding upon a human services job, people usually think about several possibilities.

3. They imagine themselves in different situations, and in so doing, they probably think about their interests, goals, and abilities.

4. Choosing among occupations in the field of human services is an important decision to make.

Which one of the following is the best arrangement of these sentences?

A. 2-4-1-3
B. 2-3-4-1
C. 4-2-1-3
D. 4-2-3-1

The correct answer to this sample question is D.

SOLUTION:

Choices A and C *present the information in the paragraph out of logical sequence. In both A and C, sentence 1 comes before sentence 3. The key element in the organization of this paragraph is that sentence 3 contains the information to which sentence 1 refers; therefore, in logical sequence, sentence 3 should come before sentence 1.*

Choice B *also presents the information in the paragraph out of logical sequence. Choice B places sentence 4 in between sentence 1 and sentence 3, thereby interrupting the logical sequence of the information in the paragraph.*

Choice D *presents the information in the paragraph in the best logical sequence. Sentence 4 introduces the main idea of the paragraph: "choosing an occupation in the field of human services." Sentences 2-3-1 then follow up on this idea by describing, in order, the steps involved in making such a choice.*

SUBJECT AREA 5

SUPERVISION: These questions test for knowledge of the principles and practices employed in planning, organizing, and controlling the activities of a work unit toward predetermined objectives. The concepts covered, usually in a situational question format, include such topics as assigning and reviewing work; evaluating performance; maintaining work standards; motivating and developing subordinates; implementing procedural change; increasing efficiency; and dealing with problems of absenteeism, morale, and discipline.

TEST TASK: You will be presented with situations in which you must apply knowledge of the principles and practices of supervision in order to answer the questions correctly.

SAMPLE QUESTION:

Assume that the unit you supervise is given a new work assignment and that you are unsure about the proper procedure to use in performing this assignment. Which one of the following actions should you take FIRST in this situation?

A. Obtain input from your staff.
B. Consult other unit supervisors who have had similar assignments.
C. Use an appropriate procedure from a similar assignment that you are familiar with.
D. Discuss the matter with your supervisor.

The correct answer to this sample question is D.

SOLUTION:

Choice A is not correct. Since this assignment is new for your unit, your staff would not be expected to be more knowledgeable than you about the proper procedure.

Choice B is not correct. Although discussing this matter with other supervisors may increase your knowledge of the new assignment, similar assignments performed in other units may differ in some important way from your new assignment. Other units may also function differently from your unit, so the procedures used to perform similar assignments may differ accordingly.

Choice C is not correct. Since this assignment is new for your unit, you would have no way of knowing whether the procedure from a similar assignment is appropriate to use. You would need someone with the appropriate knowledge, usually your supervisor, to determine if the procedure from a similar assignment could be used before you actually employed this procedure in the performance of your new assignment.

Choice D is the correct answer to this question. Your supervisor is more likely to be informed about what procedure may be appropriate for work that he or she assigns to you than would other unit supervisors or your staff. Even if your supervisor does not know what procedure is appropriate, a decision regarding which procedure to use should be made with his or her participation, since he or she has the ultimate responsibility for your unit's work.

GENERAL TEST-TAKING GUIDELINES

Read all test directions and instructions carefully. Make sure that you carefully read and follow all directions and any special instructions for the test. If sample questions are provided, do them for practice. *Make sure you understand the directions and instructions before you start to answer the questions.*

Make sure you are answering the correct test questions in the correct test booklets. The particular test you are taking may involve skipping some questions in the test booklet or may involve answering questions in more than one test booklet. You are responsible for making sure you get the right test booklets for your particular test and for determining which questions you are to answer. Refer to your test materials for information on which test booklets and questions you are to answer.

Make sure the choice you mark on your answer sheet matches the question you are answering in the test booklet. Most written multiple-choice tests are scanned and scored by machine. You will not get credit for choices you mark in the wrong place on the answer sheet. Check your work to make sure that the number of the question you are answering in the test booklet matches the choice you are marking on your answer sheet.

Make sure you record all your answers on the answer sheet. Only the answers you mark on your answer sheet will be counted toward your score.

Make sure you fill in the circles for your choices completely and carefully. Avoid making stray pencil marks on your answer sheet. The scanning machine may interpret these marks to be your answers.

HOW TO TAKE A TEST

I. YOU MUST PASS AN EXAMINATION

A. *WHAT EVERY CANDIDATE SHOULD KNOW*

Examination applicants often ask us for help in preparing for the written test. What can I study in advance? What kinds of questions will be asked? How will the test be given? How will the papers be graded?

As an applicant for a civil service examination, you may be wondering about some of these things. Our purpose here is to suggest effective methods of advance study and to describe civil service examinations.

Your chances for success on this examination can be increased if you know how to prepare. Those "pre-examination jitters" can be reduced if you know what to expect. You can even experience an adventure in good citizenship if you know why civil service exams are given.

B. *WHY ARE CIVIL SERVICE EXAMINATIONS GIVEN?*

Civil service examinations are important to you in two ways. As a citizen, you want public jobs filled by employees who know how to do their work. As a job seeker, you want a fair chance to compete for that job on an equal footing with other candidates. The best-known means of accomplishing this two-fold goal is the competitive examination.

Exams are widely publicized throughout the nation. They may be administered for jobs in federal, state, city, municipal, town or village governments or agencies.

Any citizen may apply, with some limitations, such as the age or residence of applicants. Your experience and education may be reviewed to see whether you meet the requirements for the particular examination. When these requirements exist, they are reasonable and applied consistently to all applicants. Thus, a competitive examination may cause you some uneasiness now, but it is your privilege and safeguard.

C. *HOW ARE CIVIL SERVICE EXAMS DEVELOPED?*

Examinations are carefully written by trained technicians who are specialists in the field known as "psychological measurement," in consultation with recognized authorities in the field of work that the test will cover. These experts recommend the subject matter areas or skills to be tested; only those knowledges or skills important to your success on the job are included. The most reliable books and source materials available are used as references. Together, the experts and technicians judge the difficulty level of the questions.

Test technicians know how to phrase questions so that the problem is clearly stated. Their ethics do not permit "trick" or "catch" questions. Questions may have been tried out on sample groups, or subjected to statistical analysis, to determine their usefulness.

Written tests are often used in combination with performance tests, ratings of training and experience, and oral interviews. All of these measures combine to form the best-known means of finding the right person for the right job.

II. HOW TO PASS THE WRITTEN TEST

A. NATURE OF THE EXAMINATION

To prepare intelligently for civil service examinations, you should know how they differ from school examinations you have taken. In school you were assigned certain definite pages to read or subjects to cover. The examination questions were quite detailed and usually emphasized memory. Civil service exams, on the other hand, try to discover your present ability to perform the duties of a position, plus your potentiality to learn these duties. In other words, a civil service exam attempts to predict how successful you will be. Questions cover such a broad area that they cannot be as minute and detailed as school exam questions.

In the public service similar kinds of work, or positions, are grouped together in one "class." This process is known as *position-classification*. All the positions in a class are paid according to the salary range for that class. One class title covers all of these positions, and they are all tested by the same examination.

B. FOUR BASIC STEPS

1) Study the announcement

How, then, can you know what subjects to study? Our best answer is: "Learn as much as possible about the class of positions for which you've applied." The exam will test the knowledge, skills and abilities needed to do the work.

Your most valuable source of information about the position you want is the official exam announcement. This announcement lists the training and experience qualifications. Check these standards and apply only if you come reasonably close to meeting them.

The brief description of the position in the examination announcement offers some clues to the subjects which will be tested. Think about the job itself. Review the duties in your mind. Can you perform them, or are there some in which you are rusty? Fill in the blank spots in your preparation.

Many jurisdictions preview the written test in the exam announcement by including a section called "Knowledge and Abilities Required," "Scope of the Examination," or some similar heading. Here you will find out specifically what fields will be tested.

2) Review your own background

Once you learn in general what the position is all about, and what you need to know to do the work, ask yourself which subjects you already know fairly well and which need improvement. You may wonder whether to concentrate on improving your strong areas or on building some background in your fields of weakness. When the announcement has specified "some knowledge" or "considerable knowledge," or has used adjectives like "beginning principles of…" or "advanced … methods," you can get a clue as to the number and difficulty of questions to be asked in any given field. More questions, and hence broader coverage, would be included for those subjects which are more important in the work. Now weigh your strengths and weaknesses against the job requirements and prepare accordingly.

3) Determine the level of the position

Another way to tell how intensively you should prepare is to understand the level of the job for which you are applying. Is it the entering level? In other words, is this the position in which beginners in a field of work are hired? Or is it an intermediate or advanced level? Sometimes this is indicated by such words as "Junior" or "Senior" in the class title. Other jurisdictions use Roman numerals to designate the level – Clerk I, Clerk II, for example. The word "Supervisor" sometimes appears in the title. If the level is not indicated by the title, check the description of duties. Will you be working under very close supervision, or will you have responsibility for independent decisions in this work?

4) Choose appropriate study materials

Now that you know the subjects to be examined and the relative amount of each subject to be covered, you can choose suitable study materials. For beginning level jobs, or even advanced ones, if you have a pronounced weakness in some aspect of your training, read a modern, standard textbook in that field. Be sure it is up to date and has general coverage. Such books are normally available at your library, and the librarian will be glad to help you locate one. For entry-level positions, questions of appropriate difficulty are chosen – neither highly advanced questions, nor those too simple. Such questions require careful thought but not advanced training.

If the position for which you are applying is technical or advanced, you will read more advanced, specialized material. If you are already familiar with the basic principles of your field, elementary textbooks would waste your time. Concentrate on advanced textbooks and technical periodicals. Think through the concepts and review difficult problems in your field.

These are all general sources. You can get more ideas on your own initiative, following these leads. For example, training manuals and publications of the government agency which employs workers in your field can be useful, particularly for technical and professional positions. A letter or visit to the government department involved may result in more specific study suggestions, and certainly will provide you with a more definite idea of the exact nature of the position you are seeking.

III. KINDS OF TESTS

Tests are used for purposes other than measuring knowledge and ability to perform specified duties. For some positions, it is equally important to test ability to make adjustments to new situations or to profit from training. In others, basic mental abilities not dependent on information are essential. Questions which test these things may not appear as pertinent to the duties of the position as those which test for knowledge and information. Yet they are often highly important parts of a fair examination. For very general questions, it is almost impossible to help you direct your study efforts. What we can do is to point out some of the more common of these general abilities needed in public service positions and describe some typical questions.

1) General information

Broad, general information has been found useful for predicting job success in some kinds of work. This is tested in a variety of ways, from vocabulary lists to questions about current events. Basic background in some field of work, such as sociology or economics, may be sampled in a group of questions. Often these are principles which have become familiar to most persons through exposure rather than through formal training. It is difficult to advise you how to study for these questions; being alert to the world around you is our best suggestion.

2) Verbal ability

An example of an ability needed in many positions is verbal or language ability. Verbal ability is, in brief, the ability to use and understand words. Vocabulary and grammar tests are typical measures of this ability. Reading comprehension or paragraph interpretation questions are common in many kinds of civil service tests. You are given a paragraph of written material and asked to find its central meaning.

3) Numerical ability

Number skills can be tested by the familiar arithmetic problem, by checking paired lists of numbers to see which are alike and which are different, or by interpreting charts and graphs. In the latter test, a graph may be printed in the test booklet which you are asked to use as the basis for answering questions.

4) Observation

A popular test for law-enforcement positions is the observation test. A picture is shown to you for several minutes, then taken away. Questions about the picture test your ability to observe both details and larger elements.

5) Following directions

In many positions in the public service, the employee must be able to carry out written instructions dependably and accurately. You may be given a chart with several columns, each column listing a variety of information. The questions require you to carry out directions involving the information given in the chart.

6) Skills and aptitudes

Performance tests effectively measure some manual skills and aptitudes. When the skill is one in which you are trained, such as typing or shorthand, you can practice. These tests are often very much like those given in business school or high school courses. For many of the other skills and aptitudes, however, no short-time preparation can be made. Skills and abilities natural to you or that you have developed throughout your lifetime are being tested.

Many of the general questions just described provide all the data needed to answer the questions and ask you to use your reasoning ability to find the answers. Your best preparation for these tests, as well as for tests of facts and ideas, is to be at your physical and mental best. You, no doubt, have your own methods of getting into an exam-taking mood and keeping "in shape." The next section lists some ideas on this subject.

IV. KINDS OF QUESTIONS

Only rarely is the "essay" question, which you answer in narrative form, used in civil service tests. Civil service tests are usually of the short-answer type. Full instructions for answering these questions will be given to you at the examination. But in case this is your first experience with short-answer questions and separate answer sheets, here is what you need to know:

1) Multiple-choice Questions

Most popular of the short-answer questions is the "multiple choice" or "best answer" question. It can be used, for example, to test for factual knowledge, ability to solve problems or judgment in meeting situations found at work.

A multiple-choice question is normally one of three types—

- It can begin with an incomplete statement followed by several possible endings. You are to find the one ending which *best* completes the statement, although some of the others may not be entirely wrong.
- It can also be a complete statement in the form of a question which is answered by choosing one of the statements listed.

- It can be in the form of a problem – again you select the best answer.

Here is an example of a multiple-choice question with a discussion which should give you some clues as to the method for choosing the right answer:

When an employee has a complaint about his assignment, the action which will *best* help him overcome his difficulty is to
- A. discuss his difficulty with his coworkers
- B. take the problem to the head of the organization
- C. take the problem to the person who gave him the assignment
- D. say nothing to anyone about his complaint

In answering this question, you should study each of the choices to find which is best. Consider choice "A" – Certainly an employee may discuss his complaint with fellow employees, but no change or improvement can result, and the complaint remains unresolved. Choice "B" is a poor choice since the head of the organization probably does not know what assignment you have been given, and taking your problem to him is known as "going over the head" of the supervisor. The supervisor, or person who made the assignment, is the person who can clarify it or correct any injustice. Choice "C" is, therefore, correct. To say nothing, as in choice "D," is unwise. Supervisors have and interest in knowing the problems employees are facing, and the employee is seeking a solution to his problem.

2) True/False Questions

The "true/false" or "right/wrong" form of question is sometimes used. Here a complete statement is given. Your job is to decide whether the statement is right or wrong.

SAMPLE: A roaming cell-phone call to a nearby city costs less than a non-roaming call to a distant city.

This statement is wrong, or false, since roaming calls are more expensive.

This is not a complete list of all possible question forms, although most of the others are variations of these common types. You will always get complete directions for answering questions. Be sure you understand *how* to mark your answers – ask questions until you do.

V. RECORDING YOUR ANSWERS

Computer terminals are used more and more today for many different kinds of exams.

For an examination with very few applicants, you may be told to record your answers in the test booklet itself. Separate answer sheets are much more common. If this separate answer sheet is to be scored by machine – and this is often the case – it is highly important that you mark your answers correctly in order to get credit.

An electronic scoring machine is often used in civil service offices because of the speed with which papers can be scored. Machine-scored answer sheets must be marked with a pencil, which will be given to you. This pencil has a high graphite content which responds to the electronic scoring machine. As a matter of fact, stray dots may register as answers, so do not let your pencil rest on the answer sheet while you are pondering the correct answer. Also, if your pencil lead breaks or is otherwise defective, ask for another.

Since the answer sheet will be dropped in a slot in the scoring machine, be careful not to bend the corners or get the paper crumpled.

The answer sheet normally has five vertical columns of numbers, with 30 numbers to a column. These numbers correspond to the question numbers in your test booklet. After each number, going across the page are four or five pairs of dotted lines. These short dotted lines have small letters or numbers above them. The first two pairs may also have a "T" or "F" above the letters. This indicates that the first two pairs only are to be used if the questions are of the true-false type. If the questions are multiple choice, disregard the "T" and "F" and pay attention only to the small letters or numbers.

Answer your questions in the manner of the sample that follows:

32. The largest city in the United States is
    A. Washington, D.C.
    B. New York City
    C. Chicago
    D. Detroit
    E. San Francisco

1) Choose the answer you think is best. (New York City is the largest, so "B" is correct.)
2) Find the row of dotted lines numbered the same as the question you are answering. (Find row number 32)
3) Find the pair of dotted lines corresponding to the answer. (Find the pair of lines under the mark "B.")
4) Make a solid black mark between the dotted lines.

VI. BEFORE THE TEST

Common sense will help you find procedures to follow to get ready for an examination. Too many of us, however, overlook these sensible measures. Indeed, nervousness and fatigue have been found to be the most serious reasons why applicants fail to do their best on civil service tests. Here is a list of reminders:

- Begin your preparation early – Don't wait until the last minute to go scurrying around for books and materials or to find out what the position is all about.
- Prepare continuously – An hour a night for a week is better than an all-night cram session. This has been definitely established. What is more, a night a week for a month will return better dividends than crowding your study into a shorter period of time.
- Locate the place of the exam – You have been sent a notice telling you when and where to report for the examination. If the location is in a different town or otherwise unfamiliar to you, it would be well to inquire the best route and learn something about the building.
- Relax the night before the test – Allow your mind to rest. Do not study at all that night. Plan some mild recreation or diversion; then go to bed early and get a good night's sleep.
- Get up early enough to make a leisurely trip to the place for the test – This way unforeseen events, traffic snarls, unfamiliar buildings, etc. will not upset you.
- Dress comfortably – A written test is not a fashion show. You will be known by number and not by name, so wear something comfortable.

- Leave excess paraphernalia at home – Shopping bags and odd bundles will get in your way. You need bring only the items mentioned in the official notice you received; usually everything you need is provided. Do not bring reference books to the exam. They will only confuse those last minutes and be taken away from you when in the test room.
- Arrive somewhat ahead of time – If because of transportation schedules you must get there very early, bring a newspaper or magazine to take your mind off yourself while waiting.
- Locate the examination room – When you have found the proper room, you will be directed to the seat or part of the room where you will sit. Sometimes you are given a sheet of instructions to read while you are waiting. Do not fill out any forms until you are told to do so; just read them and be prepared.
- Relax and prepare to listen to the instructions
- If you have any physical problem that may keep you from doing your best, be sure to tell the test administrator. If you are sick or in poor health, you really cannot do your best on the exam. You can come back and take the test some other time.

VII. AT THE TEST

The day of the test is here and you have the test booklet in your hand. The temptation to get going is very strong. Caution! There is more to success than knowing the right answers. You must know how to identify your papers and understand variations in the type of short-answer question used in this particular examination. Follow these suggestions for maximum results from your efforts:

1) Cooperate with the monitor

The test administrator has a duty to create a situation in which you can be as much at ease as possible. He will give instructions, tell you when to begin, check to see that you are marking your answer sheet correctly, and so on. He is not there to guard you, although he will see that your competitors do not take unfair advantage. He wants to help you do your best.

2) Listen to all instructions

Don't jump the gun! Wait until you understand all directions. In most civil service tests you get more time than you need to answer the questions. So don't be in a hurry. Read each word of instructions until you clearly understand the meaning. Study the examples, listen to all announcements and follow directions. Ask questions if you do not understand what to do.

3) Identify your papers

Civil service exams are usually identified by number only. You will be assigned a number; you must not put your name on your test papers. Be sure to copy your number correctly. Since more than one exam may be given, copy your exact examination title.

4) Plan your time

Unless you are told that a test is a "speed" or "rate of work" test, speed itself is usually not important. Time enough to answer all the questions will be provided, but this does not mean that you have all day. An overall time limit has been set. Divide the total time (in minutes) by the number of questions to determine the approximate time you have for each question.

5) Do not linger over difficult questions

If you come across a difficult question, mark it with a paper clip (useful to have along) and come back to it when you have been through the booklet. One caution if you do this – be sure to skip a number on your answer sheet as well. Check often to be sure that you have not lost your place and that you are marking in the row numbered the same as the question you are answering.

6) Read the questions

Be sure you know what the question asks! Many capable people are unsuccessful because they failed to *read* the questions correctly.

7) Answer all questions

Unless you have been instructed that a penalty will be deducted for incorrect answers, it is better to guess than to omit a question.

8) Speed tests

It is often better NOT to guess on speed tests. It has been found that on timed tests people are tempted to spend the last few seconds before time is called in marking answers at random – without even reading them – in the hope of picking up a few extra points. To discourage this practice, the instructions may warn you that your score will be "corrected" for guessing. That is, a penalty will be applied. The incorrect answers will be deducted from the correct ones, or some other penalty formula will be used.

9) Review your answers

If you finish before time is called, go back to the questions you guessed or omitted to give them further thought. Review other answers if you have time.

10) Return your test materials

If you are ready to leave before others have finished or time is called, take ALL your materials to the monitor and leave quietly. Never take any test material with you. The monitor can discover whose papers are not complete, and taking a test booklet may be grounds for disqualification.

VIII. EXAMINATION TECHNIQUES

1) Read the general instructions carefully. These are usually printed on the first page of the exam booklet. As a rule, these instructions refer to the timing of the examination; the fact that you should not start work until the signal and must stop work at a signal, etc. If there are any *special* instructions, such as a choice of questions to be answered, make sure that you note this instruction carefully.

2) When you are ready to start work on the examination, that is as soon as the signal has been given, read the instructions to each question booklet, underline any key words or phrases, such as *least, best, outline, describe* and the like. In this way you will tend to answer as requested rather than discover on reviewing your paper that you *listed without describing*, that you selected the *worst* choice rather than the *best* choice, etc.

3) If the examination is of the objective or multiple-choice type – that is, each question will also give a series of possible answers: A, B, C or D, and you are called upon to select the best answer and write the letter next to that answer on your answer paper – it is advisable to start answering each question in turn. There may be anywhere from 50 to 100 such questions in the three or four hours allotted and you can see how much time would be taken if you read through all the questions before beginning to answer any. Furthermore, if you come across a question or group of questions which you know would be difficult to answer, it would undoubtedly affect your handling of all the other questions.

4) If the examination is of the essay type and contains but a few questions, it is a moot point as to whether you should read all the questions before starting to answer any one. Of course, if you are given a choice – say five out of seven and the like – then it is essential to read all the questions so you can eliminate the two that are most difficult. If, however, you are asked to answer all the questions, there may be danger in trying to answer the easiest one first because you may find that you will spend too much time on it. The best technique is to answer the first question, then proceed to the second, etc.

5) Time your answers. Before the exam begins, write down the time it started, then add the time allowed for the examination and write down the time it must be completed, then divide the time available somewhat as follows:
    - If 3-1/2 hours are allowed, that would be 210 minutes. If you have 80 objective-type questions, that would be an average of 2-1/2 minutes per question. Allow yourself no more than 2 minutes per question, or a total of 160 minutes, which will permit about 50 minutes to review.
    - If for the time allotment of 210 minutes there are 7 essay questions to answer, that would average about 30 minutes a question. Give yourself only 25 minutes per question so that you have about 35 minutes to review.

6) The most important instruction is to *read each question* and make sure you know what is wanted. The second most important instruction is to *time yourself properly* so that you answer every question. The third most important instruction is to *answer every question*. Guess if you have to but include something for each question. Remember that you will receive no credit for a blank and will probably receive some credit if you write something in answer to an essay question. If you guess a letter – say "B" for a multiple-choice question – you may have guessed right. If you leave a blank as an answer to a multiple-choice question, the examiners may respect your feelings but it will not add a point to your score. Some exams may penalize you for wrong answers, so in such cases *only*, you may not want to guess unless you have some basis for your answer.

7) Suggestions
    a. Objective-type questions
        1. Examine the question booklet for proper sequence of pages and questions
        2. Read all instructions carefully
        3. Skip any question which seems too difficult; return to it after all other questions have been answered
        4. Apportion your time properly; do not spend too much time on any single question or group of questions

5. Note and underline key words – *all, most, fewest, least, best, worst, same, opposite*, etc.
6. Pay particular attention to negatives
7. Note unusual option, e.g., unduly long, short, complex, different or similar in content to the body of the question
8. Observe the use of "hedging" words – *probably, may, most likely*, etc.
9. Make sure that your answer is put next to the same number as the question
10. Do not second-guess unless you have good reason to believe the second answer is definitely more correct
11. Cross out original answer if you decide another answer is more accurate; do not erase until you are ready to hand your paper in
12. Answer all questions; guess unless instructed otherwise
13. Leave time for review

  b. Essay questions
    1. Read each question carefully
    2. Determine exactly what is wanted. Underline key words or phrases.
    3. Decide on outline or paragraph answer
    4. Include many different points and elements unless asked to develop any one or two points or elements
    5. Show impartiality by giving pros and cons unless directed to select one side only
    6. Make and write down any assumptions you find necessary to answer the questions
    7. Watch your English, grammar, punctuation and choice of words
    8. Time your answers; don't crowd material

8) Answering the essay question

Most essay questions can be answered by framing the specific response around several key words or ideas. Here are a few such key words or ideas:

M's: manpower, materials, methods, money, management
P's: purpose, program, policy, plan, procedure, practice, problems, pitfalls, personnel, public relations

  a. Six basic steps in handling problems:
    1. Preliminary plan and background development
    2. Collect information, data and facts
    3. Analyze and interpret information, data and facts
    4. Analyze and develop solutions as well as make recommendations
    5. Prepare report and sell recommendations
    6. Install recommendations and follow up effectiveness

  b. Pitfalls to avoid
    1. *Taking things for granted* – A statement of the situation does not necessarily imply that each of the elements is necessarily true; for example, a complaint may be invalid and biased so that all that can be taken for granted is that a complaint has been registered

2. *Considering only one side of a situation* – Wherever possible, indicate several alternatives and then point out the reasons you selected the best one
3. *Failing to indicate follow up* – Whenever your answer indicates action on your part, make certain that you will take proper follow-up action to see how successful your recommendations, procedures or actions turn out to be
4. *Taking too long in answering any single question* – Remember to time your answers properly

IX. AFTER THE TEST

Scoring procedures differ in detail among civil service jurisdictions although the general principles are the same. Whether the papers are hand-scored or graded by machine we have described, they are nearly always graded by number. That is, the person who marks the paper knows only the number – never the name – of the applicant. Not until all the papers have been graded will they be matched with names. If other tests, such as training and experience or oral interview ratings have been given, scores will be combined. Different parts of the examination usually have different weights. For example, the written test might count 60 percent of the final grade, and a rating of training and experience 40 percent. In many jurisdictions, veterans will have a certain number of points added to their grades.

After the final grade has been determined, the names are placed in grade order and an eligible list is established. There are various methods for resolving ties between those who get the same final grade – probably the most common is to place first the name of the person whose application was received first. Job offers are made from the eligible list in the order the names appear on it. You will be notified of your grade and your rank as soon as all these computations have been made. This will be done as rapidly as possible.

People who are found to meet the requirements in the announcement are called "eligibles." Their names are put on a list of eligible candidates. An eligible's chances of getting a job depend on how high he stands on this list and how fast agencies are filling jobs from the list.

When a job is to be filled from a list of eligibles, the agency asks for the names of people on the list of eligibles for that job. When the civil service commission receives this request, it sends to the agency the names of the three people highest on this list. Or, if the job to be filled has specialized requirements, the office sends the agency the names of the top three persons who meet these requirements from the general list.

The appointing officer makes a choice from among the three people whose names were sent to him. If the selected person accepts the appointment, the names of the others are put back on the list to be considered for future openings.

That is the rule in hiring from all kinds of eligible lists, whether they are for typist, carpenter, chemist, or something else. For every vacancy, the appointing officer has his choice of any one of the top three eligibles on the list. This explains why the person whose name is on top of the list sometimes does not get an appointment when some of the persons lower on the list do. If the appointing officer chooses the second or third eligible, the No. 1 eligible does not get a job at once, but stays on the list until he is appointed or the list is terminated.

X. HOW TO PASS THE INTERVIEW TEST

The examination for which you applied requires an oral interview test. You have already taken the written test and you are now being called for the interview test – the final part of the formal examination.

You may think that it is not possible to prepare for an interview test and that there are no procedures to follow during an interview. Our purpose is to point out some things you can do in advance that will help you and some good rules to follow and pitfalls to avoid while you are being interviewed.

What is an interview supposed to test?

The written examination is designed to test the technical knowledge and competence of the candidate; the oral is designed to evaluate intangible qualities, not readily measured otherwise, and to establish a list showing the relative fitness of each candidate – as measured against his competitors – for the position sought. Scoring is not on the basis of "right" and "wrong," but on a sliding scale of values ranging from "not passable" to "outstanding." As a matter of fact, it is possible to achieve a relatively low score without a single "incorrect" answer because of evident weakness in the qualities being measured.

Occasionally, an examination may consist entirely of an oral test – either an individual or a group oral. In such cases, information is sought concerning the technical knowledges and abilities of the candidate, since there has been no written examination for this purpose. More commonly, however, an oral test is used to supplement a written examination.

Who conducts interviews?

The composition of oral boards varies among different jurisdictions. In nearly all, a representative of the personnel department serves as chairman. One of the members of the board may be a representative of the department in which the candidate would work. In some cases, "outside experts" are used, and, frequently, a businessman or some other representative of the general public is asked to serve. Labor and management or other special groups may be represented. The aim is to secure the services of experts in the appropriate field.

However the board is composed, it is a good idea (and not at all improper or unethical) to ascertain in advance of the interview who the members are and what groups they represent. When you are introduced to them, you will have some idea of their backgrounds and interests, and at least you will not stutter and stammer over their names.

What should be done before the interview?

While knowledge about the board members is useful and takes some of the surprise element out of the interview, there is other preparation which is more substantive. It *is* possible to prepare for an oral interview – in several ways:

1) Keep a copy of your application and review it carefully before the interview

This may be the only document before the oral board, and the starting point of the interview. Know what education and experience you have listed there, and the sequence and dates of all of it. Sometimes the board will ask you to review the highlights of your experience for them; you should not have to hem and haw doing it.

2) Study the class specification and the examination announcement

Usually, the oral board has one or both of these to guide them. The qualities, characteristics or knowledges required by the position sought are stated in these documents. They offer valuable clues as to the nature of the oral interview. For example, if the job involves supervisory responsibilities, the announcement will usually indicate that knowledge of modern supervisory methods and the qualifications of the candidate as a supervisor will be tested. If so, you can expect such questions, frequently in the form of a hypothetical situation which you are expected to solve. NEVER go into an oral without knowledge of the duties and responsibilities of the job you seek.

3) Think through each qualification required

Try to visualize the kind of questions you would ask if you were a board member. How well could you answer them? Try especially to appraise your own knowledge and background in each area, *measured against the job sought*, and identify any areas in which you are weak. Be critical and realistic – do not flatter yourself.

4) Do some general reading in areas in which you feel you may be weak

For example, if the job involves supervision and your past experience has NOT, some general reading in supervisory methods and practices, particularly in the field of human relations, might be useful. Do NOT study agency procedures or detailed manuals. The oral board will be testing your understanding and capacity, not your memory.

5) Get a good night's sleep and watch your general health and mental attitude

You will want a clear head at the interview. Take care of a cold or any other minor ailment, and of course, no hangovers.

What should be done on the day of the interview?

Now comes the day of the interview itself. Give yourself plenty of time to get there. Plan to arrive somewhat ahead of the scheduled time, particularly if your appointment is in the fore part of the day. If a previous candidate fails to appear, the board might be ready for you a bit early. By early afternoon an oral board is almost invariably behind schedule if there are many candidates, and you may have to wait. Take along a book or magazine to read, or your application to review, but leave any extraneous material in the waiting room when you go in for your interview. In any event, relax and compose yourself.

The matter of dress is important. The board is forming impressions about you – from your experience, your manners, your attitude, and your appearance. Give your personal appearance careful attention. Dress your best, but not your flashiest. Choose conservative, appropriate clothing, and be sure it is immaculate. This is a business interview, and your appearance should indicate that you regard it as such. Besides, being well groomed and properly dressed will help boost your confidence.

Sooner or later, someone will call your name and escort you into the interview room. *This is it.* From here on you are on your own. It is too late for any more preparation. But remember, you asked for this opportunity to prove your fitness, and you are here because your request was granted.

What happens when you go in?

The usual sequence of events will be as follows: The clerk (who is often the board stenographer) will introduce you to the chairman of the oral board, who will introduce you to the other members of the board. Acknowledge the introductions before you sit down. Do not be surprised if you find a microphone facing you or a stenotypist sitting by. Oral interviews are usually recorded in the event of an appeal or other review.

Usually the chairman of the board will open the interview by reviewing the highlights of your education and work experience from your application – primarily for the benefit of the other members of the board, as well as to get the material into the record. Do not interrupt or comment unless there is an error or significant misinterpretation; if that is the case, do not hesitate. But do not quibble about insignificant matters. Also, he will usually ask you some question about your education, experience or your present job – partly to get you to start talking and to establish the interviewing "rapport." He may start the actual questioning, or turn it over to one of the other members. Frequently, each member undertakes the questioning on a particular area, one in which he is perhaps most competent, so you can expect each member to participate in the examination. Because time is limited, you may also expect some rather abrupt switches in the direction the questioning takes, so do not be upset by it. Normally, a board member will not pursue a single line of questioning unless he discovers a particular strength or weakness.

After each member has participated, the chairman will usually ask whether any member has any further questions, then will ask you if you have anything you wish to add. Unless you are expecting this question, it may floor you. Worse, it may start you off on an extended, extemporaneous speech. The board is not usually seeking more information. The question is principally to offer you a last opportunity to present further qualifications or to indicate that you have nothing to add. So, if you feel that a significant qualification or characteristic has been overlooked, it is proper to point it out in a sentence or so. Do not compliment the board on the thoroughness of their examination – they have been sketchy, and you know it. If you wish, merely say, "No thank you, I have nothing further to add." This is a point where you can "talk yourself out" of a good impression or fail to present an important bit of information. Remember, *you close the interview yourself.*

The chairman will then say, "That is all, Mr. _____, thank you." Do not be startled; the interview is over, and quicker than you think. Thank him, gather your belongings and take your leave. Save your sigh of relief for the other side of the door.

How to put your best foot forward

Throughout this entire process, you may feel that the board individually and collectively is trying to pierce your defenses, seek out your hidden weaknesses and embarrass and confuse you. Actually, this is not true. They are obliged to make an appraisal of your qualifications for the job you are seeking, and they want to see you in your best light. Remember, they must interview all candidates and a non-cooperative candidate may become a failure in spite of their best efforts to bring out his qualifications. Here are 15 suggestions that will help you:

1) Be natural – Keep your attitude confident, not cocky

If you are not confident that you can do the job, do not expect the board to be. Do not apologize for your weaknesses, try to bring out your strong points. The board is interested in a positive, not negative, presentation. Cockiness will antagonize any board member and make him wonder if you are covering up a weakness by a false show of strength.

2) Get comfortable, but don't lounge or sprawl

Sit erectly but not stiffly. A careless posture may lead the board to conclude that you are careless in other things, or at least that you are not impressed by the importance of the occasion. Either conclusion is natural, even if incorrect. Do not fuss with your clothing, a pencil or an ashtray. Your hands may occasionally be useful to emphasize a point; do not let them become a point of distraction.

3) Do not wisecrack or make small talk

This is a serious situation, and your attitude should show that you consider it as such. Further, the time of the board is limited – they do not want to waste it, and neither should you.

4) Do not exaggerate your experience or abilities

In the first place, from information in the application or other interviews and sources, the board may know more about you than you think. Secondly, you probably will not get away with it. An experienced board is rather adept at spotting such a situation, so do not take the chance.

5) If you know a board member, do not make a point of it, yet do not hide it

Certainly you are not fooling him, and probably not the other members of the board. Do not try to take advantage of your acquaintanceship – it will probably do you little good.

6) Do not dominate the interview

Let the board do that. They will give you the clues – do not assume that you have to do all the talking. Realize that the board has a number of questions to ask you, and do not try to take up all the interview time by showing off your extensive knowledge of the answer to the first one.

7) Be attentive

You only have 20 minutes or so, and you should keep your attention at its sharpest throughout. When a member is addressing a problem or question to you, give him your undivided attention. Address your reply principally to him, but do not exclude the other board members.

8) Do not interrupt

A board member may be stating a problem for you to analyze. He will ask you a question when the time comes. Let him state the problem, and wait for the question.

9) Make sure you understand the question

Do not try to answer until you are sure what the question is. If it is not clear, restate it in your own words or ask the board member to clarify it for you. However, do not haggle about minor elements.

10) Reply promptly but not hastily

A common entry on oral board rating sheets is "candidate responded readily," or "candidate hesitated in replies." Respond as promptly and quickly as you can, but do not jump to a hasty, ill-considered answer.

11) Do not be peremptory in your answers

A brief answer is proper – but do not fire your answer back. That is a losing game from your point of view. The board member can probably ask questions much faster than you can answer them.

12) Do not try to create the answer you think the board member wants

He is interested in what kind of mind you have and how it works – not in playing games. Furthermore, he can usually spot this practice and will actually grade you down on it.

13) Do not switch sides in your reply merely to agree with a board member

Frequently, a member will take a contrary position merely to draw you out and to see if you are willing and able to defend your point of view. Do not start a debate, yet do not surrender a good position. If a position is worth taking, it is worth defending.

14) Do not be afraid to admit an error in judgment if you are shown to be wrong

The board knows that you are forced to reply without any opportunity for careful consideration. Your answer may be demonstrably wrong. If so, admit it and get on with the interview.

15) Do not dwell at length on your present job

The opening question may relate to your present assignment. Answer the question but do not go into an extended discussion. You are being examined for a *new* job, not your present one. As a matter of fact, try to phrase ALL your answers in terms of the job for which you are being examined.

Basis of Rating

Probably you will forget most of these "do's" and "don'ts" when you walk into the oral interview room. Even remembering them all will not ensure you a passing grade. Perhaps you did not have the qualifications in the first place. But remembering them will help you to put your best foot forward, without treading on the toes of the board members.

Rumor and popular opinion to the contrary notwithstanding, an oral board wants you to make the best appearance possible. They know you are under pressure – but they also want to see how you respond to it as a guide to what your reaction would be under the pressures of the job you seek. They will be influenced by the degree of poise you display, the personal traits you show and the manner in which you respond.

ABOUT THIS BOOK

This book contains tests divided into Examination Sections. Go through each test, answering every question in the margin. We have also attached a sample answer sheet at the back of the book that can be removed and used. At the end of each test look at the answer key and check your answers. On the ones you got wrong, look at the right answer choice and learn. Do not fill in the answers first. Do not memorize the questions and answers, but understand the answer and principles involved. On your test, the questions will likely be different from the samples. Questions are changed and new ones added. If you understand these past questions you should have success with any changes that arise. Tests may consist of several types of questions. We have additional books on each subject should more study be advisable or necessary for you. Finally, the more you study, the better prepared you will be. This book is intended to be the last thing you study before you walk into the examination room. Prior study of relevant texts is also recommended. NLC publishes some of these in our Fundamental Series. Knowledge and good sense are important factors in passing your exam. Good luck also helps. So now study this Passbook, absorb the material contained within and take that knowledge into the examination. Then do your best to pass that exam.

EXAMINATION SECTION

EXAMINATION SECTION
TEST 1

DIRECTIONS: Each question or incomplete statement is followed by several suggested answers or completions. Select the l one that BEST answers the question or completes the statement. *PRINT THE LETTER OF THE CORRECT ANSWER IN THE SPACE AT THE RIGHT.*

1. The applicant you are interviewing is a man in his late forties who has recently lost his job and has a family of eight to support. He is very upset and tells you he does not know where he will get the money to purchase food for the family and pay the rent. He does not know what he will do if he is found not eligible for public assistance. He asks you whether you think he will be eligible. You feel the applicant has a good chance, and you think he should receive financial assistance, but you are not completely certain that he is eligible for public assistance under departmental policy.
Of the following, the BEST action for you to take is to

   A. reassure the applicant and tell him you are sure everything will be all right because there is no sense in worrying him before you know for certain that he is not eligible
   B. tell the applicant that as far as you are concerned he should receive public assistance but that you are not certain the department will go along with your recommendation
   C. tell the applicant that you are not sure that he will be found eligible for public assistance
   D. adopt a cool manner and tell the applicant that he must behave like an adult and not allow himself to become emotional about the situation

2. When conducting an interview with a client receiving public assistance, it would be LEAST important for you to try to

   A. understand the reasons for the client's statements
   B. conduct the interview on the client's intellectual level
   C. imitate the client's speech as much as possible
   D. impress the client with the agency's concern for his welfare

Questions 3-6.

DIRECTIONS: Questions 3 through 6 are to be answered SOLELY on basis of the following case history of the Foster family.

FOSTER CASE HISTORY

Form W-341-C
Rev. 3/1/03
600M-804077-S-200 (93)-245

Date: Jan. 25, 2015
Case Name: Foster
Case No. : ADC-3415968

Family Composition: Ann Foster, b. 7.23.77
Gerry b. 1.7.02
Susan b. 4.1.04
John b. 5.3.07
Joan b. 10.14.10

Mrs. Foster was widowed in June 2011 when her husband was killed in a car accident. Since that time, the family has received public assistance. Mrs. Foster has been referred for housekeeping service by the Social Service Department of Lincoln Hospital, where she is being treated in the neurology clinic. Her primary diagnosis is multiple sclerosis. The hospital reports that she is going through a period of deterioration characterized by an unsteady gait, and weakness and tremor in the limbs. At this time, her capacity to manage a household and four children is severely limited. She feels quite overwhelmed and is unable to function adequately in taking care of her home.

In addition to the medical reasons, it is advisable that a housekeeper be placed in the home as part of a total plan to avoid further family breakdown and deterioration. This deterioration is reflected by all family members. Mrs. Foster is severely depressed and is unable to meet the needs of her children, who have a variety of problems. Joan, the youngest, is not speaking, is hyperactive, and in general is not developing normally for a child her age. John is showing learning problems in school and has poor articulation. Susan was not promoted last year and is a behavior problem at home. Gerry, the oldest, is deformed due to a fire at age two. It is clear that Mrs. Foster cannot control or properly discipline her children, but even more important is the fact that she is unable to offer them the encouragement and guidance they require.

It is hoped that providing housekeeping service will relieve Mrs. Foster of the basic household chores so that she will be less frustrated and better able to provide the love and guidance needed by her children.

3. The age of the child who is described as not developing normally, hyperactive, and not speaking is

   A. 4　　　B. 7　　　C. 10　　　D. 13

4. Which of the following CANNOT be verified on the basis of the Foster Case History above?

   A. William Foster was Ann Foster's husband.
   B. Mrs. Foster has been seen in the neurology clinic at Lincoln Hospital.
   C. John Foster has trouble with his speech.
   D. The Foster family has received public assistance since June 2011.

5. The form on which the information about the Foster family is presented is known as

   A. Family Composition Form　　　B. Form Rev. 3/1/03
   C. Form W-341-C　　　D. ADC-3415968

6. According to the above case history, housekeeping service is being requested PRIMA-   6.____
RILY because

    A. no one in the family can perform the household chores
    B. Mrs. Foster suffers from multiple sclerosis and requires assistance with the household chores
    C. the children are exhibiting behavior problems resulti from the mother's illness
    D. the children have no father

7. You notice that an applicant whom you rejected for public assistance is back at the center   7.____
the following morning and is waiting to be interviewed by another worker in your group.
Of the following, the BEST approach for you to take is to

    A. inform the worker, before she interviews the applicant that you had interviewed and rejected him the previous day
    B. not inform the worker about the situation and let her make her own decision
    C. approach the applicant and tell him he was rejected for good reason and will have to leave the center immediately
    D. ask the special officer at the center to remove the applicant

8. You have just finished interviewing an applicant who has a violent temper and has dis-   8.____
played a great amount of hostility toward you during the interview. You find he is ineligible
for public assistance. Departmental policy is that all applicants are notified by mail in a
day or so of their acceptance or rejection for public assistance. However, you also have
the option, if you think it is desirable, of notifying the applicant at the interview.
Of the following, the BEST action for you to take in this case is to

    A. tell the applicant of his rejection during the interview
    B. have the applicant notified of the results of the interview by mail only
    C. ask your supervisor to inform the applicant of his rejection
    D. inform the applicant of the results of the interview, with a special patrolman at your side

9. You are interviewing a client who speaks English poorly and whose native language is   9.____
Spanish. Your knowledge of Spanish is very limited.
Of the following, the FIRST action it would be best for you to take is to

    A. try to locate a worker at the center who speaks Spanish
    B. write our your questions because it is easier for people to understand a new language when it is written rather than when it is spoken
    C. do the best you can, using hand gestures to make yourself understood
    D. tell the client to return with a friend or relative who speaks English

10. During an interview with a client of another race, he accuses you of racial prejudice and   10.____
asks for an interviewer of his own race.
Of the following, which is the BEST way to handle the situation?

    A. In a friendly manner, tell the client that eligibility is based on the regulations and the facts, not on prejudice, and ask him to continue with the interview.
    B. Explain to your supervisor that you cannot deal with someone who accuses you of prejudice, and ask your supervisor to assign the client someone of his own race.
    C. Assure the client that you will lean over backwards to treat his application favorably.

D. Tell the client that some of your friends are of his race and that you could therefore not possibly be prejudiced.

Questions 11-15.

DIRECTIONS: In order to answer Questions 11 through 15, assume that you have been asked to write a short report on the basis of the information contained in the following passage about the granting of emergency funds to the Smith family.

Mr. and Mrs. Smith, who have been receiving public assistance for the last six months, arrive at the center the morning of August 2, totally upset and anxious because they and their family have been burned out of their apartment the night before. The fire seems to have been of suspicious origin because at the time it broke out witnesses spotted two neighborhood teenagers running away from the scene. The policemen, who arrived at the scene shortly after the firemen, took down the pertinent information about the alleged arsonists.

The Smiths have spent the night with friends but now request emergency housing and emergency funds for themselves and their four children to purchase food and to replace the clothing which was destroyed by the fire. The burned-out apartment had consisted of 5 rooms and a bath, and the Smiths are now worried that they will be forced to accept smaller accommodations. Furthermore, since Mrs. Smith suffers from a heart murmur, she is worried that their new living quarters will necessitate her climbing too many stairs. Her previous apartment was a one-flight walk-up, which was acceptable.

As the worker in charge, you have studied the case, determined the amount of the emergency grant, made temporary arrangements for the Smiths to stay at a hotel, and reassured Mrs. Smith that everything possible will be done to find them an apartment which will meet with their approval.

11. Which of the following would it be BEST to include in the report as the reason for the emergency grant? 11._____

    A. The police have decided that the fire is of suspicious origin.
    B. Two neighborhood teenagers were seen leaving the fire at the Smiths'.
    C. The apartment of the Smith family has been destroyed by fire.
    D. Mrs. Smith suffers from a heart murmur and cannot climb stairs.

12. Which of the following would it be BEST to accept as verification of the fire? 12._____
    A

    A. letter from the friends with whom the Smiths stayed the previous night
    B. photograph of the fire
    C. dated newspaper clipping describing the fire
    D. note from the Smiths' neighbors

13. A report of the Smith family's need for a new apartment must be sent to the center's housing specialist. 13._____
    Which of the following recommendations for housing would be MOST appropriate?

    A. Two bedrooms, first floor walk-up
    B. Five rooms, ground floor
    C. Two-room suite, hotel with elevator
    D. Three rooms, building with elevator

14. For which of the following are the Smiths requesting emergency funds?

    A. Furniture
    B. Food
    C. A hotel room
    D. Repairs in their apartment

15. Which of the following statements provides the BEST summary of the action taken by you on the Smith case and is MOST important for inclusion in your report?

    A. Mr. and Mrs. Smith arrived upset and anxious and were reassured.
    B. It was verified that there was a fire.
    C. Temporary living arrangements were made, and the amount of the emergency grant was determined.
    D. The case was studied and a new apartment was found for the Smiths which met with their approval.

16. It is important that you remember what has happened between you and a client during an interview so that you may deliver appropriate services.
    However, the one of the following which is the MOST likely reason that taking notes during the interview may not always be a good practice is that

    A. you may lose the notes and have to go back and see the client again
    B. some clients may believe that you are not interested in what they are saying
    C. you are the only one who is likely to read the notes
    D. some clients may believe that you are not smart enough to remember what happened in the interview

17. Before an applicant seeking public assistance can be interviewed, he must fill out a complex application form which consists of eleven pages of questions requesting very detailed information.
    Of the following, the BEST time for you to review the information on the application form is

    A. before she begins to interview the applicant
    B. after she has asked the applicant a few questions to put him at ease
    C. towards the end of the interview so that she has a chance to think about the information received during the interview
    D. after the interview has been completed

Questions 18-20.

DIRECTIONS: In Questions 18 through 20, choose the lettered word which means MOST NEARLY the same as the underlined word in the sentence.

18. He needed public assistance because he was incapacitated. The word incapacitated means MOST NEARLY

    A. uneducated
    B. disabled
    C. uncooperative
    D. discharged

19. The caseworker explained to the client that signing the document was compulsory. The word compulsory means MOST NEARLY

    A. temporary
    B. required
    C. different
    D. comprehensive

20. The woman's actions did not <u>jeopardize</u> her eligibility for benefits.
    The word <u>jeopardize</u> means MOST NEARLY

    A. delay   B. reinforce   C. determine   D. endanger

20._____

KEY (CORRECT ANSWERS)

1.	C	11.	C
2.	C	12.	C
3.	A	13.	B
4.	A	14.	B
5.	C	15.	C
6.	B	16.	B
7.	A	17.	A
8.	B	18.	B
9.	A	19.	B
10.	A	20.	D

TEST 2

DIRECTIONS: Each question or incomplete statement is followed by several suggested answers or completions. Select the one that BEST answers the question or completes the statement. *PRINT THE LETTER OF THE CORRECT ANSWER IN THE SPACE AT THE RIGHT.*

Questions 1-4.

DIRECTIONS: Questions 1 through 4 are to be answered on the basis of the information given in the Fact Situation and Sample Form below.

FACT SITUATION

On October 7, 2014, John Smith (Case #ADC-U 1467912) applied and was accepted for public assistance for himself and his family. His family consists of his wife, Helen, and their children: William, age 9; John Jr., age 6; and Mary, age 2. The family has lived in a five-room apartment located at 142 West 137 Street, Manhattan, since July 18, 2008. Mr. Smith signed a 2-year lease for this apartment on July 18, 2014 at a rent of $500 per month. The maximum rental allowance for a family of this size is $420 per month. Utilities are included in this rent-controlled multiple dwelling.

Since the cost of renting this apartment is in excess of the allowable amount, the Supervising Clerk (Income Maintenance) is required to fill out a "Request for Approval of Exception to Policy for Shelter Allowance/Rehousing Expenses."

A sample of a section of this form follows.

SAMPLE FORM

REQUEST FOR APPROVAL OF EXCEPTION TO POLICY FOR SHELTER ALLOWANCE /REHOUSING EXPENSES

Case Name	Case No. or Pending		Acceptance Date	Group No.	
Present Address ZIP	Apt. No. or Location	No. of Rooms	Rent per Mo. $	Occupancy Date	
HOUSEHOLD COMPOSITION (List all persons living in the household) Column I Surname First	Col. 2 Birth-date	Col. 3 Sex	Column 4 Relation to Case Head	Column 5 Marital Status	Column 6 P. A. Status

1. Based on the information given in the Fact Situation, which one of the following should be entered in the space for *Occupancy Date?*

   A. October 7, 2014
   B. July 18, 2014
   C. July 18, 2008
   D. Unknown

2. What amount should be entered in the space labeled *Rent per Mo.* ?

   A. $500   B. $420   C. $300   D. $80

3. Based on the information given in the Fact Situation, it is IMPOSSIBLE to fill in which one of the following blanks?

   A. *Case Number or pending*
   B. *Acceptance Date*
   C. *Apt. No. or Location*
   D. *No. of Rooms*

4. Which of the following should be entered in Column 4 for Helen Smith?

   A. Wife   B. Head   C. Mother   D. Unknown

Questions 5-13.

DIRECTIONS: In Questions 5 through 13, perform the computations indicated and choose the CORRECT answer from the four choices given.

5. Add $4.34, $34.50, $6.00, $101.76, $90.67. From the result, subtract $60.54 and $10.56.

   A. $76.17   B. $156.37   C. $166.17   D. $300.37

6. Add 2,200, 2,600, 252, and 47.96.
   From the result, subtract 202.70, 1,200, 2,150, and 434.43.

   A. 1,112.83   B. 1,213.46   C. 1,341.51   D. 1,348.91

7. Multiply 1850 by .05 and multiply 3300 by .08 and then add both results.

   A. 242.50   B. 264.00   C. 333.25   D. 356.50

8. Multiply 312.77 by .04.
   Round off the result to the nearest hundredth.

   A. 12.52   B. 12.511   C. 12.518   D. 12.51

9. Add 362.05, 91.13, 347.81, and 17.46, and then divide the result by 6.
   The answer rounded off to the nearest hundredth is

   A. 138.409   B. 137.409   C. 136.41   D. 136.40

10. Add 66.25 and 15.06, and then multiply the result by 2 1/6.
    The answer is MOST NEARLY

    A. 176.18   B. 176.17   C. 162.66   D. 162.62

11. Each of the following options contains three decimals. In which case do all three decimals have the same value?

    A. .3; .30; .03
    B. .25; .250; .2500
    C. 1.9; 1.90; 1.09
    D. .35; .350; .035

12. Add 1/2 the sum of (539.84 and 479.26) to 1/3 the sum of (1461.93 and 927.27). 12._____
    Round off the result to the nearest whole number.

    A. 3408   B. 2899   C. 1816   D. 1306

13. Multiply $5,906.09 by 15%, and then divide the result by 1/3. 13._____

    A. $295.30   B. $885.91   C. $8,859.14   D. $29,530.45

Questions 14-18.

DIRECTIONS: Questions 14 through 18 are to be answered SOLELY on the basis of the information provided in the following passage.

The ideal relationship for the interview is one of mutual confidence. To try to pretend, to put on a front of cordiality and friendship is extremely unwise for the interviewer because he will certainly convey, by subtle means, his real feelings. It is the interviewer's responsibility to take the lead in establishing a relationship of mutual confidence.

As the interviewer, you should help the interviewee to feel at ease and ready to talk. One of the best ways to do this is to be at ease yourself. If you are, it will probably be evident; if you are not, it will almost certainly be apparent to the interviewee.

Begin the interview with topics for discussion which are easy to talk about and non-menacing. This interchange can be like the conversation of people when they are waiting for a bus, at the ball game, or discussing the weather. However, do not prolong this warm-up too long since the interviewee knows as well as you do that these are not the things he came to discuss. Delaying too long in getting down to business may suggest to him that you are reluctant to deal with the topic.

Once you get onto the main topics, do all that you can to get the interviewee to talk freely with as little prodding from you as possible. This will probably require that you give him some idea of the area, and of ways of looking at it. Avoid, however, prejudicing or coloring his remarks by what you say; especially, do not in any way indicate that there are certain things you want to hear, others which you do not want to hear. It is essential that he feel free to express his own ideas unhampered by your ideas, your values and preconceptions.

Do not appear to dominate the interview, nor have even the suggestion of a patronizing attitude. Ask some questions which will enable the interviewee to take pride in his knowledge. Take the attitude that the interviewee sincerely wants the interview to achieve its purpose. This creates a warm, permissive atmosphere that is most important in all interviews.

14. Of the following, the BEST title for the above passage is 14._____

    A. PERMISSIVENESS IN INTERVIEWING
    B. INTERVIEWING TECHNIQUES
    C. THE FACTOR OF PRETENSE IN THE INTERVIEW
    D. THE CORDIAL INTERVIEW

15. Which of the following recommendations on the conduct of an interview is made by the above passage?
    A. Conduct the interview as if it were an interchange between people discussing the weather.
    B. The interview should be conducted in a highly impersonal manner.
    C. Allow enough time for the interview so that the interviewee does not feel rushed.
    D. Start the interview with topics which are not threatening to the interviewee.

16. The above passage indicates that the interviewer should
    A. feel free to express his opinions
    B. patronize the interviewee and display a permissive attitude
    C. permit the interviewee to give the needed information in his own fashion
    D. provide for privacy when conducting the interview

17. The meaning of the word *unhampered*, as it is used in the last sentence of the fourth paragraph of the preceding passage, is MOST NEARLY
    A. unheeded   B. unobstructed
    C. hindered   D. aided

18. It can be INFERRED from the above passage that
    A. interviewers, while generally mature, lack confidence
    B. certain methods in interviewing are more successful than others in obtaining information
    C. there is usually a reluctance on the part of interviewers to deal with unpleasant topics
    D. it is best for the interviewer not to waiver from the use of hard and fast rules when dealing with clients

19. The applicant whom you are interviewing is not talking rationally, and he admits that he is under the influence of alcohol.
    Which of the following is the BEST way of handling this situation?
    A. Call a security guard and have the applicant removed.
    B. Tell the applicant that unless he gets control of himself, he will not receive financial assistance.
    C. Send out for a cup of black coffee for the applicant.
    D. End the interview and plan to schedule another appointment.

20. During an interview, an applicant who has submitted an application for assistance breaks down and cries. Of the following, the BEST way of handling this situation is to
    A. end the interview and schedule a new appointment
    B. be patient and sympathetic, and encourage the applicant to continue the interview
    C. tell the applicant sternly that crying will not help matters
    D. tell the applicant that you will do everything you can to get the application approved

KEY (CORRECT ANSWERS)

1. C
2. A
3. C
4. A
5. C

6. A
7. D
8. D
9. C
10. B

11. B
12. D
13. A
14. B
15. D

16. C
17. B
18. B
19. D
20. B

EXAMINATION SECTION
TEST 1

DIRECTIONS: Each question or incomplete statement is followed by several suggested answers or completions. Select the one that BEST answers the question or completes the statement. *PRINT THE LETTER OF THE CORRECT ANSWER IN THE SPACE AT THE RIGHT.*

1. Assume that an applicant, obviously under a great deal of stress, talks continuously and rambles, making it difficult for you to determine the exact problem and her need. In order to make the interview more successful, it would be BEST for you to
    A. interrupt the applicant and ask her specific questions in order to get the information you need
    B. tell the applicant that her rambling may be a basic cause of her problem
    C. let the applicant continue talking as long as she wishes
    D. ask the applicant to get to the point because other people are waiting for you

1.____

2. A worker must be able to interview clients all day and still be able to listen and maintain interest.
Of the following, it is MOST important for you to show interest in the client because, if you appear interested,
    A. the client is more likely to appreciate your professional status
    B. the client is more likely to disclose a greater amount of information
    C. the client is less likely to tell lies
    D. you are more likely to gain your supervisor's approval

2.____

3. The application process is overwhelming to applicant Ms. M. She is very anxious and is fearful that she does not have all that she needs to be eligible for assistance. As a result, every time she is asked to produce a verifying document during the interview, she fumbles and drops all the other documents to the floor.
Of the following, the MOST effective method for you to use to complete the application process is to
    A. ask Ms. M not to be so nervous because you cannot get the work done if she fusses so much
    B. take the documents away from Ms. M and do it your self
    C. suggest that Ms. M get a friend to come and help her with the papers
    D. try to calm Ms. M and tell her that you are willing to help her with the papers to get the information you require

3.____

4. An applicant for public assistance claims that her husband deserted the family and that she needs money immediately for food since her children have not eaten for two days. Under normal procedure, she has to wait several days before she can be given any money for this purpose. In accordance with departmental policy, no exception can be made in this case.
Of the following, the BEST action for you to take is to
   A. tell her that, according to departmental policy, she cannot be given money immediately
   B. purchase some food for her, using your own funds, so that she can feed her children
   C. take up a collection among co-workers
   D. send her to another center

5. Applicants for public assistance often complain about the length of the application form. They also claim that the questions are too personal, since all they want is money. It is true that the form is long, but the answers to all the questions on the form are needed so that the department can make a decision on eligibility.
When applicants complain, which of the following would be the MOST appropriate action for you to take?
   A. Help such applicants understand that each question has a purpose which will help in the determination of eligibility
   B. Tell such applicants that you agree but that you must comply with regulations because it is your job
   C. Tell such applicants that they should stop complaining if they want you to help
   D. Refer such applicants to a supervisor who will explain agency policy

6. Which one of the following statements BEST describes the primary goal of a worker?
   A. Process as many clients in as short a time as possible
   B. Help his clients
   C. Grow into a more understanding person
   D. Assert his authority

7. Restating a question before the person being interviewed gives an answer to the original question is usually NOT good practice *principally* because
   A. the client will think that you don't know your job
   B. it may confuse the client
   C. the interviewer should know exactly what to ask and how to put the question
   D. it reveals the interviewer's insecurity

8. A white worker can BEST improve his ability to work with black clients if he
   A. tries to forget that the clients are black
   B. tells the black clients that he has no prejudices
   C. becomes aware of the problems black clients face
   D. socializes with black workers in the agency

9. A client warns that if he does not get what he wants he will report you to your supervisor and, if necessary, to the mayor's office.
Of the following, the MOST appropriate response for you to make in this situation is to
   A. encourage the client to do as he threatens because you know that you are right
   B. call your supervisor in so that the client may confront him
   C. explain to the client how the decision will be made on his request and suggest what action he can take if there is an adverse decision
   D. try to understand the client's problem but tell him that he must not explode in the office because you will have to ask him to leave if he does

Questions 10-20.

DIRECTIONS: Refer to the following Semi-Monthly Family Allowance Schedule and Conversion Table when answering Questions 10 through 20.

SEMI-MONTHLY FAMILY ALLOWANCE SCHEDULE
(Based on Number of Persons in Household)

NUMBER OF PERSONS IN HOUSEHOLD						
One	Two	Three	Four	Five	Six	Each Additional Person
$470.00	$750.00	$1000.00	$1290.00	$1590.00	$1840.00	$25.00

CONVERSION TABLE - WEEKLY TO SEMI-MONTHLY AMOUNTS

DOLLARS				CENTS			
Weekly Amount	Semi-Monthly Amount	Weekly Amount	Semi-Monthly Amount	Weekly Amount	Semi-Monthly Amount	Weekly Amount	Semi-Monthly Amount
$10.00	$21.70	$510.00	$1105.00	$0.10	$0.20	$5.10	$11.10
20.00	43.30	520.00	1126.70	0.20	0.40	5.20	11.30
30.00	65.00	530.00	1148.30	0.30	0.70	5.30	11.50
40.00	86.70	540.00	1170.00	0.40	0.90	5.40	11.70
50.00	108.30	550.00	1191.70	0.50	1.10	5.50	11.90
60.00	130.00	560.00	1213.30	0.60	1.30	5.60	12.10
70.00	151.70	570.00	1235.00	0.70	1.50	5.70	12.40
80.00	173.30	580.00	1256.70	0.80	1.70	5.80	12.60
90.00	195.00	590.00	1278.30	0.90	2.00	5.90	12.80
100.00	216.70	600.00	1300.00	1.00	2.20	6.00	13.00
110.00	238.30	610.00	1321.70	1.10	2.40	6.10	13.20
120.00	260.00	620.00	1343.30	1.20	2.60	6.20	13.40
130.00	281.70	630.00	1365.00	1.30	2.80	6.30	13.70
140.00	303.30	640.00	1386.70	1.40	3.00	6.40	13.90
150.00	325.00	650.00	1408.30	1.50	3.30	6.50	14.10
160.00	346.70	660.00	1430.00	1.60	3.50	6.60	14.30
170.00	368.30	670.00	1451.70	1.70	3.70	6.70	14.50
180.00	390.00	680.00	1473.30	1.80	3.90	6.80	14.70
190.00	411.70	690.00	1495.00	1.90	4.10	6.90	15.00
200.00	433.30	700.00	1516.70	2.00	4.30	7.00	15.20
210.00	455.00	710.00	1538.30	2.10	4.60	7.10	15.40
220.00	476.70	720.00	1560.00	2.20	4.80	7.20	15.60
230.00	498.30	730.00	1581.70	2.30	5.00	7.30	15.80
240.00	520.00	740.00	1603.30	2.40	5.20	7.40	16.00
250.00	541.70	750.00	1625.00	2.50	5.40	7.50	16.30
260.00	563.30	760.00	1646.70	2.60	5.60	7.60	16.50
270.00	585.00	770.00	1668.30	2.70	5.90	7.70	16.70
280.00	606.70	780.00	1690.00	2.80	6.10	7.80	16.90
290.00	628.30	790.00	1711.70	2.90	6.30	7.90	17.10
300.00	650.00	800.00	1733.30	3.00	6.50	8.00	17.30
310.00	671.70	810.00	1755.00	3.10	6.70	8.10	17.60
320.00	693.30	820.00	1776.70	3.20	6.90	8.20	17.80
330.00	715.00	830.00	1798.30	3.30	7.20	8.30	18.00
340.00	736.70	840.00	1820.00	3.40	7.40	8.40	18.20
350.00	783.00	850.00	1841.70	3.50	7.60	8.50	18.40
360.00	780.00	860.00	1863.30	3.60	7.80	8.60	18.60
370.00	801.70	870.00	1885.00	3.70	8.00	8.70	18.90
380.00	823.30	880.00	1906.70	3.80	8.20	8.80	19.10
390.00	845.00	890.00	1928.30	3.90	8.50	8.90	18.30
400.00	866.70	900.00	1950.00	4.00	8.70	9.00	19.50
410.00	888.30	910.00	1971.70	4.10	8.90	9.10	19.70
420.00	910.00	920.00	1993.30	4.20	9.10	9.20	19.90
430.00	931.70	930.00	2015.00	4.30	9.30	9.30	20.20
440.00	953.30	940.00	2036.70	4.40	9.50	9.40	20.40
450.00	975.00	950.00	2058.30	4.50	9.80	9.50	20.60
460.00	996.70	960.00	2080.00	4.60	10.00	9.60	20.80
470.00	1018.30	970.00	2101.70	4.70	10.20	9.70	21.00
480.00	1040.00	980.00	2123.30	4.80	10.40	9.80	21.20
490.00	1061.70	990.00	2145.00	4.90	10.60	9.90	21.50
500.00	1083.30	1000.00	2166.70	5.00	10.80		

NOTE: Questions 10 through 20 are to be answered SOLELY on the basis of the Schedule and Table given above and the information and case situations given below.

Questions 10 through 14 are based on Case Situation #1.
Questions 15 through 20 are based on Case Situation #2.

Public assistance grants are computed on a semi-monthly basis. This means that all figures are first broken down into semi-monthly amounts, and that when a client receives a check twice a month, each semi-monthly check covers his requirements for a period of approximately 2-1/6 weeks. The grants are computed by means of the following procedures.

1. Determine the semi-monthly allowance for the family from the Semi-Monthly Family Allowance Schedule.
2. Determine total semi-monthly income by deducting from the semi-monthly gross earnings (the wages or salary *before* payroll deductions) all semi-monthly expenses for federal, state, and city income taxes, Social Security payments, State Disability Insurance payments, union dues, cost of transportation, and $10.00 per work day for lunch.
3. Add the semi-monthly allowance and the semi-monthly rent (monthly rent must be divided in half).
4. Subtract the semi-monthly income (if there is any income).
5. The formula for computing the semi-monthly grant is:
   Family Allowance + Rent (semi-monthly)
   Total Income   (semi-monthly)
   = Amount of Grant   (semi-monthly)
6. Refer to the Conversion Table in order to convert weekly amounts into semi-monthly amounts.

CASE SITUATION #1

The Smiths receive public assistance. The family includes John Smith, his wife Barbara, and their four children. They occupy a five-room apartment for which the rent is $1050.00 per month. Mr. Smith is employed as a cleaner and his gross wages are $1000 per week. He is employed 5 days a week and spends $7.00 a day carfare. He buys his lunches. The following weekly deductions are made from his salary:

Social Security	$60.00
Disability Benefits	3.80
Federal Income Tax	43.00
State Income Tax	28.00
City Income Tax	10.00

CASE SITUATION #2

The Jones family receives public assistance. The family includes Steven and Diane Jones and their two children. They occupy a four-room apartment for which the rental is $850.00 a month. Mr. Jones is employed as a handyman, and his gross wages are $900 per week. He is employed 4 days a week and spends $7.00 a day carfare. He buys his lunches. He has the following weekly deductions made from his salary:

Social Security	$40.00
Disability Benefits	2.70
Federal Income Tax	38.90
State Income Tax	20.50
City Income Tax	6.20

10. The weekly amount that Mr. Smith contributes towards Social Security, Disability Benefits, and income taxes is
    A. $313.70 B. $231.40 C. $144.80 D. $106.80

11. The semi-monthly family allowance for the Smith family is
    A. $1290.00 B. $1590.00 C. $1840.00 D. $1845.00

12. What is the total of semi-monthly expenses related to Mr. Smith's employment which will be deducted from semi-monthly gross earnings to compute semi-monthly income?
    A. $497.80 B. $422.00 C. $389.50 D. $229.80

13. Which of the following amounts is the total semi-monthly income for the Smith family?
    A. $2166.70 B. $2000.00 C. $1668.90 D. $1004.40

14. The amount of the grant which the Smith family is entitled to receive is
    A. $2365.00 B. $1840.00 C. $1392.20 D. $696.10

15. The weekly amount that Mr. Jones contributes towards Social Security, Disability Benefits, and income taxes is
    A. $108.30 B. $176.30 C. $234.30 D. $234.70

16. The semi-monthly family allowance for the Jones family is
    A. $750.00 B. $1000.00 C. $1220.00 D. $1290.00

17. The total of semi-monthly expenses related to Mr. Jones' employment which will be deducted from semi-monthly gross earnings is
    A. $172.30 B. $189.30 C. $382.00 D. $407.20

18. Which of the following amounts is the total semi-monthly income for the Jones family? 18.____
    A. $1282.00   B. $1553.20   C. $1568.00   D. $2122.30

19. The grant which the Jones family will receive is 19.____
    A. $147.00   B. $294.00   C. $1290.00   D. $1715.00

20. If Mrs. Jones' monthly rent had been $1050, what would the amount of the grant be? 20.____
    A. $247.00   B. $494.00   C. $772.00   D. $1822.00

KEY (CORRECT ANSWERS)

1. A
2. B
3. D
4. A
5. A

6. B
7. B
8. C
9. C
10. C

11. C
12. A
13. C
14. D
15. A

16. D
17. C
18. C
19. A
20. A

TEST 2

DIRECTIONS: Each question or incomplete statement is followed by several suggested answers or completions. Select the one that BEST answers the question or completes the statement. *PRINT THE LETTER OF THE CORRECT ANSWER IN THE SPACE AT THE RIGHT.*

Questions 1-5.

DIRECTIONS: Each of Questions 1 through 5 consists of information given in outline form and four sentences labeled A, B, C, and D. For each question, choose the one sentence which CORRECTLY expresses the information given in outline form and which also displays PROPER English usage.

1. Client's Name - Joanna Jones
   Number of Children - 3
   Client's Income - None
   Client's Marital Status - Single
   - A. Joanna Jones is an unmarried client with three children who have no income.
   - B. Joanna Jones, who is single and has no income, a client she has three children.
   - C. Joanna Jones, whose three children are clients, is single and has no income.
   - D. Joanna Jones, who has three children, is an unmarried client with no income.

   1.___

2. Client's Name - Bertha Smith
   Number of Children - 2
   Client's Rent - $1050 per month
   Number of Rooms- 4
   - A. Bertha Smith, a client, pays $1050 per month for her four rooms with two children.
   - B. Client Bertha Smith has two children and pays $1050 per month for four rooms.
   - C. Client Bertha Smith is paying $1050 per month for two children with four rooms.
   - D. For four rooms and two children, Client Bertha Smith pays $1050 per month.

   2.___

3. Name of Employee - Cynthia Dawes
   Number of Cases Assigned - 9
   Date Cases Were Assigned - 12/16
   Number of Assigned Cases Completed - 8
   - A. On December 16, employee Cynthia Dawes was assigned nine cases; she has completed eight of these cases.
   - B. Cynthia Dawes, employee on December 16, assigned nine cases, completed eight.
   - C. Being employed on December 16, Cynthia Dawes completed eight of nine assigned cases.
   - D. Employee Cynthia Dawes, she was assigned nine cases and completed eight, on December 16.

   3.___

4. Place of Audit - Broadway Center
   Names of Auditors - Paul Cahn, Raymond Perez
   Date of Audit - 11/20
   Number of Cases Audited - 41
   - A. On November 20, at the Broadway Center 41 cases was audited by auditors Paul Cahn and Raymond Perez.
   - B. Auditors Raymond Perez and Paul Cahn has audited 41 cases at the Broadway

   4.___

       Center, on November 20.
- C. At the Broadway Center, on November 20, auditors Paul Cahn and Raymond Perez audited 41 cases.
- D. Auditors Paul Cahn and Raymond Perez at the Broadway Center, on November 20, is auditing 41 cases.

5. Name of Client - Barbra Levine   5._____
    Client's Monthly Income - $2100
    Client's Monthly Expenses - $4520
- A. Barbra Levine is a client, her monthly income is $2100 and her monthly expenses is $4520.
- B. Barbra Levine's monthly income is $2100 and she is a client, with whose monthly expenses are $4520.
- C. Barbra Levine is a client whose monthly income is $2100 and whose monthly expenses are $4520.
- D. Barbra Levine, a client, is with a monthly income which is $2100 and monthly expenses which are $4520.

Questions 6-10.

DIRECTIONS: Questions 6 through 10 are to be answered SOLELY on the basis of the information contained in the following passage.

    Any person who is living in New York City and is otherwise eligible may be granted public assistance whether or not he has New York State residence. However, since New York City does not contribute to the cost of assistance granted to persons who are without State residence, the cases of all recipients must be formally identified as to whether or not each member of the household has State residence.

    To acquire State residence a person must have resided in New York State continuously for one year. Such residence is not lost unless the person is out of the State continuously for a period of one year or longer. Continuous residence does not include any period during which the individual is a patient in a hospital, an inmate of a public institution or of an incorporated private institution, a resident on a military reservation or a minor residing in a boarding home while under the care of an authorized agency. Receipt of public assistance does not prevent a person from acquiring State residence. State residence, once acquired, is not lost because of absence from the State while a person is serving in the U.S. Armed Forces or the Merchant Marine; nor does a member of the family of such a person lose State residence while living with or near that person in these circumstances.

    Each person, regardless of age, acquires or loses State residence as an individual. There is no derivative State residence except for an infant at the time of birth. He is deemed to have State residence if he is in the custody of both parents and either one of them has State residence, or if the parent having custody of him has State residence.

6. According to the above passage, an infant is deemed to have New York State residence at the time of his birth *if*
    A. he is born in New York State but neither of his parents is a resident
    B. he is in the custody of only one parent, who is not a resident, but his other parent is a resident
    C. his brother and sister are residents
    D. he is in the custody of both his parents but only one of them is a resident

7. The Jones family consists of five members. Jack and Mary Jones have lived in New York State continuously for the past eighteen months after having lived in Ohio since they were born. Of their three children, one was born ten months ago and has been in the custody of his parents since birth. Their second child lived in Ohio until six months ago and then moved in with his parents. Their third child had never lived in New York until he moved with his parents to New York eighteen months ago. However, he entered the armed forces one month later and has not lived in New York since that time.
    Based on the above passage, how many members of the Jones family are New York State residents?
    A. 2   B. 3   C. 4   D. 5

8. Assuming that each of the following individuals has lived continuously in New York State for the past year, and has never previously lived in the State, which one of them is a New York State resident?
    A. Jack Salinas, who has been an inmate in a State correctional facility for six months of the year
    B. Fran Johnson, who has lived on an Army base for the entire year
    C. Arlene Snyder, who married a non-resident during the past year
    D. Gary Phillips, who was a patient in a Veterans Administration hospital for the entire year

9. The above passage implies that the reason for determining whether or not a recipient of public assistance is a State resident is that
    A. the cost of assistance for non-residents is not a New York City responsibility
    B. non-residents living in New York City are not eligible for public assistance
    C. recipients of public assistance are barred from acquiring State residence
    D. New York City is responsible for the full cost of assistance to recipients who are residents

10. Assume that the Rollins household in New York City consists of six members at the present time - Anne Rollins, her three children, her aunt and her uncle. Anne Rollins and one of her children moved to New York City seven months ago. Neither of them had previously lived in New York State. Her other two children have lived in New York City continuously for the past two years, as has her aunt. Anne Rollins' uncle had lived in New York City continuously for many years until two years ago. He then entered the armed forces and has returned to New York City within the past month.
    Based on the above passage, how many members of the Rollins' household are New York State residents?
    A. 2   B. 3   C. 4   D. 6

11. You are interviewing a client to determine whether financial assistance should be continued and you find that what he is telling you does not agree exactly with your records.
    Of the following, the BEST way to handle this situation is to
    A. recommend that his public assistance payments be stopped, since you have caught him lying to you
    B. tell the client about the points of disagreement and ask him if he can clear them up
    C. give the client the benefit of the doubt and recommend continuation of his payments
    D. show the client the records and warn him that he must either tell the truth or lose his benefits

12. An applicant for public assistance gets angry at some of the questions you must ask her.
    Of the following, the BEST way to handle this situation is to
    A. assume that she is trying to hide something, and end the interview
    B. skip the questions that bother her and come back to them at the end of the interview
    C. tell her that she must either answer the question or leave
    D. explain to her that you are required to get answers to all the questions in order to be able to help her

13. At the end of an interview to determine whether financial assistance should be continued, the client offers to take you to lunch.
    Of the following, the BEST response to such an invitation is to
    A. tell the client that you do not take bribes and report the matter to your supervisor
    B. accept the invitation if you have the time, but do not let it influence your recommendation as to his eligibility for continuing public assistance
    C. politely refuse the invitation, and do not let it influence your recommendation as to his continuing eligibility for public assistance
    D. point out to the client that his budget does not include money for entertainment

Questions 14-18.

DIRECTIONS: Questions 14 through 18 are to be answered SOLELY on the basis of the information, the assumptions, and the table given below.

Each question describes an applicant family. You are to determine into which of the four categories (A, B, C, or D) each of the applicant families should be placed. In order to do this, you must match the description of the applicant family with the factors determining eligibility for each of the four categories. Each applicant family must meet ALL of the criteria for the category.

ASSUMPTIONS FOR ALL QUESTIONS

The information in the following tables does NOT necessarily reflect actual practice in the Department of Social Services.
1. The date of application is January 25.
   Each applicant family that cannot be placed in categories A, B, or C must be placed in category D.
2. A *dependent child* is a child who is less than 18 years of age, or less than 21 years of age if attending school full time, who depends upon its parents for support.
3. A mother in a family with one or more dependent children is not expected to work and her work status is not to be considered in establishing the category of the family.

5 (#2)

CATEGORY OF APPLICANT FAMILY	FACTORS DETERMINING ELIGIBILITY

A	1. There is at least one dependent child in the home.
	2. Children are deprived of parental support because father is:
	    (a) Deceased
	    (b) Absent from the home
	    (c) Incapacitated due to medically verified illness
	    (d) Over age 65
	    (e) Not fully employed because of verified ill health
	3. Parents or guardians reside in the same home as the children.
	4. Applicant family must have resided in the State for a period of one year or more.

B	1. There is at least one dependent child in the home. 2. Both parents are in the home and are not incapacitated. 3. Both parents are the children's natural parents. 4. Father unemployed or works less than 70 hours per month. 5. Father has recent work history. 6. Father not currently receiving Unemployment Insurance Benefits. 7. Father available and willing to work. 8. Applicant family must have resided in the State for a period of one year or more.
C	1. There is a war veteran in the home. 2. Applicant families do not meet the criteria for Categories A or B.
D	Applicant families do not meet the criteria for Categories A, B, or C

14. Woman, aged 52, with child 6 years old who she states was left in her home at the age of 2. Woman states child is her niece, and that she has no knowledge of whereabouts of parents or any other relatives. Both woman and child have resided in the State since June 15.   14. ___

15. Married couple with 2 dependent children at home. Family has resided in the State for the last 5 years. Wife cannot work. Husband, veteran of Gulf War, can work only 15 hours a week due to kidney ailment (verified).   15. ___

16. Married couple, both aged 35, with 3 dependent children at home, 1 of whom is 17 years of age. Wife available for work and presently working 2 days a week, 7 hours each day. Husband, who was laid off two weeks ago, is not eligible for Unemployment Insurance Benefits. Family has resided in the State since January 1, 2002.

17. Married couple with 1 dependent child at home. They have resided in the State since January 25, 2001. Wife must remain home to take care of child. Husband veteran of Gulf War. Husband is available for work on a limited basis because of heart condition which has been verified. A second child, a married 17-year-old son, lives in California.

18. Married couple with 2 children, ages 6 and 12, at home. Family has resided in the State since June 2, 1998. Wife not available for work. Husband, who served in the Iraqi War, was laid off 3 weeks ago and is receiving Unemployment Insurance Benefits of $500.00 weekly.

19. Of the following, the MOST important reason for referring a public assistance client for employment or training is to
    A. give him self-confidence
    B. make him self-supporting
    C. have him learn a new trade
    D. take him off the streets

20. Sometimes clients become silent during interviews.
    Of the following, the MOST probable reason for such silence is that the client is
    A. getting ready to tell a lie
    B. of low intelligence and does not know the answers to your questions
    C. thinking things over or has nothing more to say on the subject
    D. wishing he were not on welfare

KEY (CORRECT ANSWERS)

1. D	6. D	11. B	16. B
2. B	7. B	12. D	17. A
3. A	8. C	13. C	18. C
4. C	9. A	14. D	19. B
5. C	10. C	15. A	20. C

EXAMINATION SECTION
TEST 1

DIRECTIONS: Each question or incomplete statement is followed by several suggested answers or completions. Select the one the BEST answers the question or completes the statement. *PRINT THE LETTER OF THE CORRECT ANSWER IN THE SPACE AT THE RIGHT.*

1. Assuming the absence of any other disqualifying factor, which of the following would be eligible for Transitional Child Care?
    I. Vernon, age 32, a single father of a 12-year-old daughter, who has just been hired at a new job and previously received Family Assistance. The state income standard is $1000 a month; his income at the new job will be $1800 a month.
    II. Carol, age 45, a single mother of two children, ages 2 and 6. She has not received public assistance in more than a year, but recent pay cuts have dropped her below the poverty level.
    III. Robert, age 48, a single father of a 14-year-old daughter, who received family assistance until being hired to work as a clerk at a law firm. The state income standard is $1000 a month; his income at the new job will be $1500 a month.

    A. I only
    B. I and II
    C. II and III
    D. I, II and III

2. A family's standard of need for their area is $419 per month. To pass the gross income test and therefore qualify for income disregards, the family's gross monthly income cannot exceed $_____.

    A. 419.00
    B. 628.50
    C. 775.15
    D. 838.00

3. The Welfare Reform Act of 1997 mandates that all applicants or recipients aged _____ or over must submit to screening for the presence of an alcohol or substance abuse problem.

    A. 13
    B. 15
    C. 18
    D. 21

4. The "Work First" goal of the Welfare Reform Act of 1997 is typically set aside when the client
    I. is a victim of domestic violence and working or participating in work activities may place him/her in danger
    II. is the single parent of one or more children under the age of 3
    III. has a significant disability and is applying for federal SSI

    A. I only   B. I and III   C. II and III   D. I, II and III

5. A woman who is pregnant is eligible for Family Assistance

   A. as soon as the pregnancy is medically verified
   B. after the first trimester
   C. after the second trimester
   D. as soon as the child is born

6. A Temporary Assistance recipient, a single mother, has been sanctioned for not complying with the alcohol/illegal substance screening requirements of her benefit agreement. After official sanction, the consequence for this recipient is a

   A. $50 deduction from monthly cash assistance payments
   B. 25% reduction in her monthly cash assistance payment
   C. total disqualification from benefits
   D. total disqualification from benefits and criminal prosecution, it can be determined that the client is using an illegal substance

7. Generally, minors who are at least _____ years old can have a Temporary Assistance case opened in their own name.

   A. 13   B. 16   C. 17   D. 18

8. Pregnant women are exempted from work requirements under workfare programs

   A. throughout their entire pregnancy
   B. after the first trimester
   C. after the second trimester
   D. after the eighth month

9. For a single parent with a dependent child younger than 6, the minimum number of weekly work hours required for Temporary Assistance benefits would be

   A. 10
   B. 20
   C. 30
   D. 40

10. For the second time since beginning to Family Assistance benefits, a recipient fails to comply with the work requirements of her program. Typically, benefits will be suspended for a period of no less than _____.

    A. 30 days
    B. 90 days
    C. 3 months
    D. 6 months

11. A single mother receiving Family Assistance benefits consistently fails to cooperate with the local social services district in establishing the legal father of her child. Typically, the consequence for this failure to cooperate is a

    A. $50 monthly deduction in monthly benefits per each child
    B. 25% reduction in monthly benefits
    C. 50% reduction in monthly benefits
    D. total suspension of benefits

12. A mother and her two children receive Family Assistance. Her grant includes $291 for basic needs, a shelter voucher of $205.00, and a fuel/utility voucher of $54—for a total benefit of $550.00. Recently, the mother received a notice from the Department of Social Services, stating that last year they paid the gas & electric company more than her utility allowance. Under typical conditions, the Department will deduct $ _____ from the mother's monthly grant until the overpayment is repaid.

    A. $5.40
    B. $11.00
    C. $55.00
    D. $82.50

13. In general, income disregards for Family Assistance recipients are only applied if wages are reported within _____ of receipt of income.

    A. 48 hours
    B. 5 days
    C. 10 days
    D. 30 days

14. During their first year of residence in New York, U.S. citizens who have relocated to the state

    A. are not eligible for any type of state-funded assistance
    B. receive 50 percent of the New York State benefit or the benefit paid by their prior state of residence, whichever is greater
    C. receive a pro rata benefit that is scaled according to their time of residence
    D. receive the same benefits as any other resident of New York who is a full U.S. citizen

15. The 60-month time limit for Family Assistance would usually apply to a

    A. family with two working parents whose combined income still falls below the poverty test
    B. minor child who lives in a family currently receiving Family Assistance
    C. single-parent family in which the parent is temporarily unable to work due to injury
    D. grandmother who is caring for a child and receiving aid only for the child's needs

16. For applicants of Family Assistance, the add-on rate disregard (47% as of 2002) only applies if the applicant received temporary assistance in one of the _____ months prior to application.

    A. 2   B. 4   C. 6   D. 9

17. A recipient of Family Assistance has failed to comply with his work requirements, and has received notice from the Department of Social Services warning him of this. Generally, the recipient has a period of _____ days in which to provide reasons for this failure, and thereby put and end to the sanctioning process.

    A. 3
    B. 7
    C. 10
    D. 15

18. Which of the following may be denied Temporary Assistance because they refuse to live at home with their parents?

    I.   single individuals between 18 and 21 who are not married, are not pregnant, and who have no children, if their parents offer to support them in their home
    II. single individuals between 18 and 21 who unmarried and childless, but pregnant, if their parents offer to support them in their home
    III. single parents between 18 and 21, if their parents offer to support them in their home
    IV. married parents between 18 and 21, if the parents of one offer to support them in their home

    A. I only
    B. I and II
    C. I, II, and III
    D. I, II, III and IV

19. A family has two children enrolled in Learnfare. In the previous academic quarter, each of the children had six unexcused absences from school. Under typical circumstances, the family will be penalized with a

    A. one-time $120 deduction from the monthly benefit
    B. total loss of benefits for one month
    C. $120 deduction from benefits for a period of three months
    D. total loss of benefits for a period of three months

20. Generally, no Temporary Assistance benefits will be given for a minor child who is absent or expected to be absent from a household for more than _____ days without good cause.

    A. 10
    B. 45
    C. 90
    D. 180

21. As of 2002, which of the following resources was NOT exempt from the consideration of an applicant's eligibility for Safety Net Assistance?

    A. A home
    B. $2000 in liquid assets
    C. Standard personal deduction from federal income tax
    D. A car valued up to $4650

22. If a family passes the gross income test for earned income disregards, which of the following would be included in the family's calculated income?

    I. The first $50 spent each month on child support
    II. For six months, the earnings of a child who is a full-time student
    III. For six months, income from a child's participation in a job training program
    IV. A $1000 inheritance from a recently deceased relative

    A. I only
    B. II and III
    C. IV only
    D. I, II, III and IV

23. As of 2002, agencies paying out Safety Net Assistance must have _____ percent of their single-parent caseload meet established work requirements.

    A. 25
    B. 35
    C. 50
    D. 75

24. Under the law, the Department of Social Services in a given area may take up to _____ to issue Expedited Food Stamps to families that qualify.

    A. 24 hours
    B. 48 hours
    C. 7 days
    D. 10 days

25. The state time limit on a client's receipt of cash Safety Net Assistance is _____ months.

    A. 6
    B. 15
    C. 24
    D. 60

KEY (CORRECT ANSWERS)

1. A
2. C
3. C
4. B
5. A

6. B
7. B
8. D
9. B
10. C

11. B
12. C
13. C
14. B
15. A

16. B
17. C
18. A
19. C
20. B

21. C
22. C
23. C
24. C
25. C

TEST 2

DIRECTIONS: Each question or incomplete statement is followed by several suggested answers or completions. Select the one the BEST answers the question or completes the statement. *PRINT THE LETTER OF THE CORRECT ANSWER IN THE SPACE AT THE RIGHT.*

1. Compared to the previous state welfare system, programs under the Welfare Reform Act of 1997 generally
    I. provide more limited special needs and emergency grants
    II. place more recipients into workfare, and for more hours
    III. use more non-cash aid in lieu of cash aid
    IV. provide more generous income disregards

    A. I and II
    B. II and IV
    C. II, III and IV
    D. I, II, III and IV

    1._____

2. In general, temporary assistance will not be given to an unmarried person under 18 who is not attending school, or who does not have a diploma/GED, unless the person is supporting a child

    A. younger than 12 weeks old
    B. younger than 1 year
    C. younger than 3 years
    D. under 18

    2._____

3. Which of the following would be eligible for Family Assistance benefits?

    A. A family of three which includes a father who suffers from alcoholism
    B. A family of four in which a 19-year-old student is receiving income from a work-study program
    C. A family of five who has already received 60 months of Family Assistance coverage
    D. Immigrant families who arrived in the United States after August 22, 1996.

    3._____

4. The earned income disregards for Family Assistance recipients would apply to
    I. Social Security income
    II. Veterans' benefits
    III. gifts from relatives
    IV. revenues from the sale of an automobile

    A. I and II
    B. II only
    C. III and IV
    D. I, II, III and IV

    4._____

5. Temporary Assistance benefits are usually NOT given for a minor child who is absent—or expected to be absent—from a household for a prescribed period of time without good cause. "Good cause" would include
    I. placement in foster care (as long as return to the home is the goal)
    II. attendance at a distant school
    III. extended hospitalization, if return is expected
    IV. living with a close relative

    A. I only
    B. I, II, and III
    C. II and IV
    D. I, II, III and IV

    5._____

6. A single person is generally NOT eligible for Temporary Assistance if his or her work experience consists of

   A. child care for another person who provides community service
   B. work in the non-profit sector, if no public or private for-profit work is available
   C. subsidized public-sector employment
   D. unsubsidized employment

7. Once an applicant for Temporary Assistance receives a notice of a disability determination, he or she typically has _____ days from the receipt of this notice to request a hearing on the matter.

   A. 5
   B. 10
   C. 30
   D. 90

8. A single person receiving Safety Net assistance qualifies for an earned income disregard. If the person earns $400 a month, and the poverty level for her region and status is $600, the amount of her disregard is $ _____. Assume an add-on rate of 45%.

   A. 90.00
   B. 180.00
   C. 245.00
   D. 270.00

9. Safety Net Assistance recipients who reach the time limit for cash benefits, or who fall into other eligibility categories, receive primarily noncash assistance, including direct vendor payments or two-party checks for rent and utilities. Of the remaining SNA grants to these recipients, about _____ percent will be accessible only through an electronic transfer system.

   A. 20
   B. 40
   C. 60
   D. 80

10. A child enrolled in the Learnfare program must attend school with no more than four unexcused absences during an academic quarter. Usually, an absence will be unexcused if it is due to
    I. a court appearance
    II. a suspension
    III. the child's having to care for a younger sibling
    IV. a family vacation

    A. I and II   B. II and III
    C. III and IV   D. I, II, III and IV

11. A household of three has monthly gross earnings of $1080. The standard of need for the household is $664 per month. The household passes both the gross income test and the poverty level test, because the poverty level for the area and status is $1081.66. With an add-on rate of 45%, the family would qualify for a monthly grant of $_____ after earned income disregards.

    A. 90
    B. 119.50
    C. 222.33
    D. 544.50

12. A Safety Net Assistance recipient, a single man without dependents, has been sanctioned for not complying with the substance abuse treatment requirements of his benefit agreement. After official sanction, the consequence for this recipient is a

    A. $50 monthly deduction from his basic needs benefit
    B. 25% deduction from his overall benefit, including vouchers
    C. total disqualification from benefits
    D. total disqualification from benefits and criminal prosecution, if the substance being abused is illegal

13. The work requirements of state Temporary Assistance programs would be MOST likely to apply to a

    A. person whose presence is required in the home because of the incapacity of another member of the household
    B. person aged 60 or older
    C. 22-year-old who has enrolled as a full-time student at a technical college
    D. single parent caring for a child under a year old, for a 3-month period

14. A Safety Net Assistance recipient may possibly be included in the work participation rates of an agency's program if he or she participates in
    I. community service
    II. unsubsidized employment
    III. attendance in a GED program
    IV. workfare

    A. I and II
    B. II only
    C. II, III and IV
    D. I, II, III and IV

15. A single recipient in Safety Net Assistance has had rent and utilities paid out of his allowance, and received small cash payments equaling about $1 a day for the month. There is still about $29 left in the recipient's allowance. Under the law, this remainder will be paid

    A. to the recipient in cash, but deducted from the next allowance
    B. to the recipient in cash
    C. through an electronic card that can be used to purchase goods and services
    D. back to the social services agency

16. Typically, a person receiving restricted cash Safety Net Assistance will receive a small percentage of the grant in cash. This portion of the benefit is the _____ allowance

    A. personal needs
    B. investment
    C. shelter
    D. utilities

17. Generally, all household members who are applying for Food Stamp benefits must register for employment at the time of application, EXCEPT for members who are working a minimum of _____ hours per week.

    A. 10
    B. 15
    C. 21
    D. 30

18. Mr. Douglas, a Family Assistance recipient, beings working at a job that earns him a gross monthly salary of $400 a month, well below the poverty level. Under the 2002 add-on rate of 47%, his "countable" monthly income would be $ _____.

    A. 90.00
    B. 164.00
    C. 188.00
    D. 212.00

19. Of the following, those eligible for cash Safety Net Assistance include a
    I. single-parent families in which the parent is abusing marijuana
    II. 17-year-old girl without children who has no adult relative to live with
    III. household that has received Family Assistance for a total of 60 months
    IV. family in which the head of the household fails to comply with drug and alcohol screening requirements

    A. I and IV
    B. II only
    C. II and III
    D. I, II, III and IV

20. Generally, a family may qualify for Expedited Food Stamps if they have no liquid resources and their gross monthly income is less than $ _____.

    A. 150.00
    B. 250.00
    C. 300 or 50% less than the poverty level, whichever is highest
    D. 500.00

21. A recipient of Safety Net Assistance fails to attend several consecutive meetings at an outpatient drug rehabilitation center. Because this is the first time he has failed to comply with the drug treatment requirements of the program,

    A. he will be warned by the agency that further failures will result in a suspension of benefits
    B. his benefits will be suspended for no less than 45 days
    C. his benefits will be suspended for no less than 180 days
    D. he will be removed from the caseload

22. Federal Food Stamp benefits

    A. involve an eligibility level that is generally higher than state Temporary Assistance levels
    B. involve an eligibility level that is generally lower than state Temporary Assistance levels
    C. are automatically terminated once an individual leaves Temporary Assistance
    D. are terminated only if the person's 60-month time limit for Temporary Assistance have expired

23. For a single parent with a 10-year-old dependent child, the number of minimum weekly work hours required for compliance with Temporary Assistance would generally be

    A. 10
    B. 20
    C. 30
    D. 40

24. Generally, the review of a client's eligibility for Temporary Assistance takes place every _____ months.

    A. 3
    B. 6
    C. 18
    D. 30

25. Generally, a single mother's Temporary Assistance benefits are NOT suspended or discontinued if he or she

    A. fails to accept a job offer
    B. refuses to sign a lien on real property that he/she owns
    C. fails to apply for SSI, Unemployment insurance or other available benefits
    D. aids the Child Support Enforcement Unit in establishing paternity for a child born out of wedlock

KEY (CORRECT ANSWERS)

1.	C	11.	B
2.	A	12.	C
3.	B	13.	C
4.	C	14.	D
5.	B	15.	C
6.	A	16.	A
7.	B	17.	D
8.	A	18.	B
9.	D	19.	B
10.	C	20.	A

21. B
22. A
23. C
24. B
25. D

EXAMINATION SECTION
TEST 1

DIRECTIONS: Each question or incomplete statement is followed by several suggested answers or completions. Select the one that BEST answers the question or completes the statement. *PRINT THE LETTER OF THE CORRECT ANSWER IN THE SPACE AT THE RIGHT.*

1. For a worker to give a client advice based upon what the worker would do in a like situation is generally

    A. *good* practice, principally because it forms a very realistic and human basis for advice
    B. *good* practice, principally because it provides the wisest counsel the worker can give generating from his sympathetic understanding
    C. *poor* practice, principally because it leads the worker into a relationship with the client on a personal level rather than on the more desirable impersonal, professional level
    D. *poor* practice, principally because the client's point of view and motivation may be different from the worker's

2. For a worker to reassure a client by stating, *"Everything is going to be all right,"* when the worker is aware that everything cannot possibly be all right and that practical help with the client's problem will not be forthcoming for a long time would generally be a

    A. *good* idea, since a client should be shielded as much as possible, for the duration of the crisis period, from the negative factors in a situation
    B. *good* idea, since the worker should be using a supporting relationship to carry out his role as a helping person
    C. *poor* idea, since it does not portray reality and may result in resentment on the part of the client
    D. *poor* idea, since it will develop a feeling of dependence on the part of the client, thus impairing a basic tool of the professional worker

3. For a worker to finish a sentence for a client who appears to be groping for words when the worker believes he knows what the client wishes to say would generally be

    A. *advisable,* because it facilitates efficient interviewing and aids the client in verbalizing
    B. *advisable,* because it tends to reduce client embarrassment and develop good rapport and mutual understanding between client and worker
    C. *inadvisable,* because it tends to undermine the client's self-reliance and ability to think independently
    D. *inadvisable,* because the client may have wished to say something else and may be too embarrassed or fearful of displeasing to point this out

4. When interviewing an applicant who is resistive to the extent that the information he gives in answer to the investigator's questions is incomplete and obscure, a worker should FIRST

    A. attempt to understand the character of the applicant and uncover the reasons for his attitude

B. ignore the applicant's attitude and get whatever information she can from him
C. inform the applicant that concealing relevant facts concerning his case is a basis for prosecution for perjury
D. request the applicant to leave and to return when he is in a better frame of mind

5. After analyzing the information obtained about a client, the worker tells him, *"The reason why you keep quitting jobs is that you think maybe you won't do a good job and will be fired."*
For the worker to tell this to a client would generally be

   A. *advisable,* as long as the analysis is well-conceived and based upon a sufficient amount of reliable information
   B. *advisable,* if the statement is prefaced by, "On the basis of the information I have, I am convinced that...." since any such analysis is subject to the possibility of error
   C. *inadvisable,* since for greatest usefulness the client should be brought by the discussion to the point where he himself arrives at the explanation for his conduct
   D. *inadvisable,* since the focus of the worker's attention and worker-client relationships should be on effects, not on causes

6. Contact with a client over a period of time involves the worker in a relationship which can lead either to an expression by the client of a direct positive feeling of being accepted or understood, or to an indirect negative response such as breaking subsequent appointments, refusal to talk, etc.
When faced with such a negative response from a client, the worker should realize that

   A. he has failed to use a professional approach to the client
   B. negative, as well as positive, responses are to be expected from most clients
   C. the client is out of touch with reality
   D. there is no significance to such a response and should, therefore, be ignored by the worker

7. The practice of casework in a social agency or institution involves working with a number of clients with a range of problems which confront them in varying life situations.
To say that all cases are psycho-social in nature means that

   A. agency function is the sole determinant of the caseworker's focus
   B. all cases encompass both objective reality and the meaning of reality to the client experiencing it
   C. all casework practice is a form of psychotherapy
   D. equal weighting must be given to psychological and social factors in every case

8. Diagnosis in casework is a process whereby the caseworker strives to determine the underlying causes and contributing factors to the client's social maladjustment.
It is important to have such diagnosis PRIMARILY because

   A. the client may not feel his problems are properly understood unless he is involved in the diagnostic process
   B. unless the underlying causes are treated by the caseworker the client cannot be effectively helped
   C. the diagnostic process may reveal serious psychological pathology that requires treatment by a psychiatrist
   D. it enables the caseworker to establish casework goals that the client can realistically reach

9. When a recipient of public assistance is offered a job which will not pay enough to allow him to get off the relief rolls, he may consider several factors.
   Of the following, the factor to which a client who is a marginal worker, frequently out of work and frequently receiving either partial or full public assistance, is likely to give most consideration in deciding whether to attempt to evade taking the job is

   A. his increased status in the community when it is known that he is partially self-supporting
   B. his moral obligation to be self-supporting
   C. whether all his increased expenses will be allowed for when his new budget is determined
   D. whether the work will provide him with satisfaction

10. In professional casework, the individual is helped to take : appropriate responsibility for the solution of his own problems. The personal and social adjustment of the individual and its implications for society are stressed. This implies that the professional caseworker

    A. discourages the client from accepting help in order to protect him from feelings of dependency
    B. emphasizes to the client the need for conforming to social standards
    C. recognizes that he has to take over for the client in the solution of his problems as long as he comes to the agency
    D. uses social and psychological methods and techniques based on an assessment of a client's needs and strengths in order to effect change

11. When the worker is aware that her client is grappling with a problem, trying to solve it in a way which social workers would generally consider to be ill-advised, it would usually be BEST for the worker to

    A. maintain an understanding and accepting attitude without involving himself in finding a solution to the problem
    B. point out to the client the most desirable solution to the problem and persuade her to employ this solution
    C. point out to the client the most desirable solution to the problem, but make no effort at persuasion
    D. point out to the client the various alternative solutions to the problem and the implications of each

12. Some time ago, it was proposed that families receiving public assistance might make satisfactory foster parents.
    The current status of this proposal is that the plan

    A. has been tried out but did not prove successful largely because the foster parents felt little incentive to continue the burdens of foster parenthood
    B. is now being tried out and is so far working out despite the fact that there is no material incentive to the families to being foster parents
    C. is now being tried out, its prospects for success aided by the fact that the allowances for the foster child are larger than the normal public assistance allowance
    D. is still receiving serious consideration and is expected to be tried out once certain legal and psychological problems have been overcome

13. The Department of Welfare makes a distinction between an abandoned child and a foundling. Both the abandoned child and the foundling have been deserted by his parent or parents, but the abandoned child is

    A. born in wedlock, while a foundling is born out-of-wedlock
    B. deserted after the age of two years, while a foundling is deserted shortly after birth
    C. of unknown identity, while a foundling is left with a note or some other identification
    D. one about whose parents something is known, while a foundling's parents are of unknown identity

14. An applicant for public assistance comes to the intake section of a welfare center. His only assets consist of $36 weekly from unemployment insurance benefits and $54 monthly from a veteran disability allowance.
    For the social investigator to include both sources of income in determining the applicant's need for public assistance would usually be

    A. *correct*, because both unemployment insurance benefits and veteran disability allowances are considered as income in estimating an applicant's needs
    B. *correct*, because only in cases of totally disabled veterans are veteran disability allowances not considered as income in estimating an applicant's needs
    C. *incorrect*, because unemployment insurance benefits are based on former taxed earnings of the applicant and are, therefore, not considered as income in estimating the applicant's needs
    D. *incorrect*, because veteran disability allowances are outright federal grants and are, therefore, not considered as income in estimating an applicant's needs

15. A payment of both principal and interest is due on money owed to a finance company by a client receiving supplementary assistance who has no available resource to meet this debt.
    The one of the following circumstances which is MOST likely to motivate the Department of Welfare to make an allowance to pay this debt is that

    A. a television set and various similar household furnishings may be repossessed
    B. garnishee action is threatened which might result in loss of employment
    C. the debt was contracted before the client was accepted for public assistance, and the Credit Clearance Unit has determined that the interest rate is not higher than the prevailing rate
    D. the debt was contracted during the period when the client was receiving public assistance

16. A recipient of Old Age Assistance notifies his social investigator that he expects to leave town for a two-months' visit with his daughter in Vermont.
    For the social investigator to tell the client that he will lose assistance during the period would be

    A. *correct*; recipients of public assistance must be discouraged from taking costly trips except in cases of visits to extremely ill, very close relatives
    B. *correct*; the recipient may lose all rights to receive assistance if he leaves the state for a period exceeding one month

C. *incorrect*; the recipient may continue to receive assistance if temporarily absent from his legal residence (for a period up to six months) if he cannot meet his needs and is otherwise eligible
D. *incorrect*; the recipient will receive assistance from the State of Vermont during that period, under a mutual assistance law between the two states

17. The one of the following which MOST accurately describes the usual manner in which the city, state, and federal governments meets the costs of the Home Relief program is that

    A. the city and the state share the cost, while the federal government makes no contribution
    B. the city pays the whole cost with no reimbursement from the state or federal government
    C. the city, state, and federal governments share the cost
    D. the state and federal government share the cost, reimbursing the city for its initial outlay

18. The Secretary of Health, Education and Welfare has, within the past several years, issued a series of administrative decisions, one of which relates to income earned by children who are recipients of public assistance.
Of the following, the MOST significant change in this respect is that income earned by children may be disregarded in computing the family welfare budget if it is

    A. earned through part-time employment of a child under 16 years of age
    B. set aside towards the child's future needs such as education and preparation for employment
    C. used for any purpose of the child or his family which is not deemed to be frivolous or otherwise undesirable
    D. utilized for current uses such as school expenses, extra clothing, and transportation needed for employment

19. *"The practice of casework cannot be learned by intellectual processes alone. Some of the most conspicuous failures each year are persons who have acquired a knowledge of human mechanisms but who, because of a faulty emotional setup, are either unable to relate this knowledge to an understanding of people in trouble or --- worse still --- because of their own needs, use their knowledge sadistically and to the harm of the client."*
According to the above paragraph, it would be LEAST correct to state with regard to skill in the field of social work that

    A. a faulty emotional set-up may result in a worker's failure to relate his knowledge to an understanding of people in trouble
    B. among the most unsuccessful social workers are some who have been educated to know and understand people and what causes them to function as they do
    C. by using intellectual processes alone, one cannot learn the practice of casework
    D. emotionally motivated, rather than intellectually gifted, people cannot in the long run be successful social caseworkers

20. Employee A is asked a question by Employee B concerning a matter which is B's responsibility primarily. Although A is not certain of the correct answer, he gives one to the best of his knowledge, not indicating his uncertainty. A's action was

    A. *acceptable*; B has the primary responsibility in this matter and is probably only seeking A's informal opinion
    B. *acceptable*; the desire for complete certainty before making a decision leads to useless delay
    C. *not acceptable*; A should have refused to answer B's question since the matter is B's responsibility primarily
    D. *not acceptable*; B may take action on the basis of the uncertain knowledge provided by A

21. A social worker who has problems centered around his acceptance of authority is MOST likely to find it difficult to

    A. relate to people
    B. adhere to agency policies
    C. develop self-awareness in handling clients
    D. cooperate with other services in helping the client

22. In the supervision of young, inexperienced investigators, the MOST important training task for the supervisor is to

    A. encourage investigators to make their own decisions about case problems
    B. give experience-based answers to various problems that arise in cases
    C. teach investigators how to analyze and assess important facts in order to make decisions about case problems
    D. teach investigators how to recognize evidence of mental breakdown

23. In order to be BEST able to teach a newly appointed employee who must learn to do a type of work which is unfamiliar to him, his supervisor should realize that during this first stage in the learning process, the subordinate is generally characterized by

    A. acute consciousness of self
    B. acute consciousness of subject matter, with little interest in persons or personalities
    C. inertness or passive acceptance of assigned role
    D. understanding of problems without understanding of the means of solving them

24. The MOST accurate of the following principles of education and learning for a supervisor to keep in mind when planning a training program for the assistant supervisors under her supervision is that

    A. assistant supervisors, like all other individuals, vary in the rate at which they learn new material and in the degree to which they can retain what they do learn
    B. experienced assistant supervisors who have the same basic college education and agency experience will be able to learn new material at approximately the same rate of speed
    C. the speed with which assistant supervisors can learn new material after the age of forty is half as rapid as at ages twenty to thirty
    D. with regard to any specific task, it is easier and takes less time to break an experienced assistant supervisor of old, unsatisfactory work habits than it is to teach him new, acceptable ones

7 (#1)

25. Assume that you are a case supervisor and that you are planning to train a group of experienced social investigators in certain specific skills which they need in their daily work.
The one of the following methods which may generally be expected to be MOST valuable in ascertaining the effectiveness of the training program is to

   A. administer an objective examination to these investigators prior to conducting the training program and an equivalent form of the examination after the program and compare the results
   B. evaluate and compare the work records of these investigators with regard to these skills prior to and after completion of the training program
   C. hold a staff meeting with the investigators after the training program is completed and allow them to discuss frankly their opinions of the values they derived from the various parts of the training
   D. prepare an objective and detailed questionnaire covering the program, have the investigators answer without identifying themselves, and analyze the answers given

25.____

26. A supervisor has received orders for a work assignment to be carried out by his unit. He has firmly decided on methods for carrying out this assignment which he believes will lead to its completion both properly and expeditiously. He has no intention whatsoever of changing his mind. After he has reached his decision, he calls a staff conference to discuss various alternative methods of carrying out the assignments without making clear that he has already decided upon the method to be used.
To hold a conference of this type would generally be a

   A. *good* idea, because his subordinates are likely to carry the assignment through better if they believe that they devised the methods used
   B. *good* idea, because the staff will have the opportunity and be properly motivated to gain knowledge and experience in methodology without endangering staff performance
   C. *poor* idea, because it would be a failure on the part of the supervisor to show the firm leadership which his unit has a right to expect
   D. *poor* idea, because the discovery by the staff that they had not actually participated in deciding upon methods to be used would have an adverse effect upon their morale

26.____

27. Supervisors are frequently faced with the necessity of training old employees in new tasks. An employee inexperienced in a task is much more likely to make a mistake than one who is experienced in it.
In delegating authority to an old employee to perform a new task, a supervisor should generally

   A. delegate the authority as soon as the subordinate gains minimum competence, allowing him to make mistakes which will not do major damage to the client or to the agency program
   B. delegate the authority as soon as the subordinate gains minimum competence, but supervise him closely, enough so that he will not have the opportunity to make even minor mistakes
   C. make the delegation of authority dependent upon the importance which the client places upon the problems involved

27.____

45

D. grant the authority until the employee has become experienced in performing the task

28. A supervisor has been transferred from supervision of one group of units to another group of units in the same center. She spends the first three weeks in her new assignment in getting acquainted with her new subordinates, their caseload problems, and their work. In this process, she notices that some of the case records and forms which are submitted to her by two of the assistant supervisors are carelessly or improperly prepared.
The BEST of the following actions for the supervisor to take in this situation is to

   A. carefully check the work submitted by these assistant supervisors during an additional three weeks before taking any more positive action
   B. confer with these offending workers and show each one where her work needs improvement and how to go about achieving it
   C. institute an in-service training program specifically designed to solve such a problem and instruct the entire subordinate staff in proper work methods
   D. make a note of these errors for documentary use in preparing the annual service rating reports and advise the workers involved to prepare their work more carefully

29. A supervisor, who was promoted to this position a year ago, has supervised a certain assistant supervisor for this one year. The work of the assistant supervisor has been very poor because he has done a minimum of work, refused to take sufficient responsibility, been difficult to handle, and required very close supervision. Apparently due to the increasing insistence by his supervisor that he improve the caliber of his work, the assistant supervisor tenders his resignation, stating that the demands of the job are too much for him. The opinion of the previous supervisor, who had supervised this assistant supervisor for two years, agrees substantially with that of the new supervisor. Under such circumstances, the BEST of the following actions the supervisor can take, in general, is to

   A. recommend that the resignation be accepted and that he be rehired should he later apply when he feels able to do the job
   B. recommend that the resignation be accepted and that he not be rehired should he later so apply
   C. refuse to accept the resignation but try to persuade the assistant supervisor to accept psychiatric help
   D. refuse to accept the resignation, promising the assistant supervisor that he will be less closely supervised in the future since he is now so experienced

30. After completing a conference with a case supervisor concerning the ramifications of a complex family problem, a social investigator informs the case supervisor that she feels that her assistant supervisor is too strict in her handling of all the social investigators under her supervision, especially in comparison with the other assistant supervisors in the center.
The one of the following actions which is generally BEST for the case supervisor to take is to

   A. advise the investigator in a friendly fashion to apply for a transfer to a unit which has a more lenient supervisor
   B. caution the investigator that complaining about a fellow employee behind her back is frowned upon by higher authority as it is a sign of disloyalty

C. inform the investigator that she, the case supervisor, will investigate the complaint to determine whether or not it has any validity
D. tell the investigator that the closer and stricter a supervisor is, the better and more completely trained will be her subordinate staff

31. Rumors have arisen to the effect that one of the social investigators under your supervision has been attending classes at a local university during afternoon hours when he is supposed to be making field visits.
The BEST of the following ways for you to approach this problem is to

    A. disregard the rumors since, like most rumors, they probably have no actual foundation in fact
    B. have a discreet investigation made in order to determine the actual facts prior to taking any other action
    C. inform the investigator that you know what he has been doing and that such behavior is an overt dereliction of duty and is punishable by dismissal
    D. review the investigator's work record, spot check his cases, and take no further action unless the quality of his work is below average for the unit

32. A supervisor must consider many factors in evaluating a worker whom he has supervised for a considerable time. In evaluating the capacity of such a worker to use independent judgment, the one of the following to which the supervisor should generally give MOST consideration is the worker's

    A. capacity to establish good relationships with people (clients, colleagues)
    B. educational background
    C. emotional stability
    D. the quality and judgment shown by the investigator in previous work situations known to the supervisor

33. A supervisor is conducting a special meeting with the assistant supervisors under her supervision to read and discuss some major complex changes in the rules and procedures. She notices that one of the assistant supervisors who is normally attentive at meetings seems to be paying no attention to what is being said. The supervisor stops reading the rules and asks the assistant supervisor a couple of questions about the changed procedure, to which she gets satisfactory answers.
The BEST action of the following for the supervisor to take at the meeting is to

    A. advise the assistant supervisor gently but firmly that these changes are complex and that her undivided attention is required in order to fully comprehend them
    B. avoid further embarrassment to the assistant supervisor by asking the group as a whole to pay more attention to what is being read
    C. discontinue the questioning and resume reading the procedure
    D. politely request the assistant supervisor to stop giving those present the impression that she is uninterested in what goes on about her

34. A supervisor becomes aware that one of her very competent experienced workers never takes notes during an interview with a client, except to note an occasional name, address, or date. When asked about this practice by the supervisor, the worker states that she has a good memory for important details and has always been able to satisfactorily record an interview after the client has left.
It would generally be BEST for the supervisor to handle this situation by

A. discussing with her that more extensive note-taking may sometimes be desirable with a client who believes note-taking to be evidence that his problem will receive serious consideration
B. agreeing with this practice since note-taking interferes with the establishment of a proper worker-client relationship
C. explaining that since interviewing is an art form rather than an exact science, a good worker must devise her own personal rules for interviewing and not be bound by general principles
D. warning the worker that memory is too uncertain a, thing to be relied upon and, therefore, notes should be taken during an interview of all matters

35. When an experienced subordinate who has the authority and information necessary to make a decision on a certain difficult matter brings the matter to his supervisor without having made the decision, it would generally be BEST for the supervisor to

    A. agree to make the decision for the subordinate after the subordinate has explained why he finds it difficult to make the decision and after he has made a recommendation
    B. make the decision for the subordinate, explaining to him the reasons for arriving at the decision
    C. refuse to make the decision, but discuss the various alternatives with the subordinate in order to clarify the issues involved
    D. refuse to make the decision, explaining to the subordinate that he is deemed to be fully qualified and competent to make the decision

36. The one of the following instances when it is MOST important for an upper level supervisor to follow the chain of command is when he is

    A. communicating decisions   B. communicating information
    C. receiving suggestions   D. seeking information

37. Experts in the field of personnel relations feel that it is generally a bad practice for subordinate employees to become aware of pending or contemplated changes in policy or organizational set-up via the *grapevine* CHIEFLY because

    A. evidence that one or more responsible officials have proved untrustworthy will undermine confidence in the agency
    B. the information disseminated by this method is seldom entirely accurate and generally spreads needless unrest among the subordinate staff
    C. the subordinate staff may conclude that the administration feels the staff cannot be trusted with the true information
    D. the subordinate staff may conclude that the administration lacks the courage to make an unpopular announcement through official channels

38. In order to maintain a proper relationship with a worker who is assigned to staff rather than line functions, a line supervisor should

    A. accept all recommendations of the staff worker
    B. include the staff worker in the conferences called by the supervisor for his subordinates
    C. keep the staff worker informed of developments in the area of his staff assignment
    D. require that the staff worker's recommendations be communicated to the supervisor through the supervisor's own superior

39. Of the following, the GREATEST disadvantage of placing a worker in a staff position under the direct supervision of the supervisor whom he advises is the possibility that the

    A. staff worker will tend to be insubordinate because of a feeling of superiority over the supervisor
    B. staff worker will tend to give advice of the type which the supervisor wants to hear or finds acceptable
    C. supervisor will tend to be mistrustful of the advice of a worker of subordinate rank
    D. supervisor will tend to derive little benefit from the advice because to supervise properly, he should know at least as much as his subordinate

40. One factor which might be given consideration in deciding upon the optimum span of control of a supervisor over his immediate subordinates is the position of the supervisor in the hierarchy of the organization. It is generally considered proper that the number of subordinates immediately supervised by a higher, upper echelon, supervisor

    A. is unrelated to and tends to form no pattern with the number supervised by lower level supervisors
    B. should be about the same as the number supervised by a lower level supervisor
    C. should be larger than the number supervised by a lower level supervisor
    D. should be smaller than the number supervised by a lower level supervisor

41. An important administrative problem is how precisely to define the limits on authority that is delegated to subordinate supervisors.
    Such definition of limits of authority should be

    A. as precise as possible and practicable in all areas
    B. as precise as possible and practicable in areas of function, but should allow considerable flexibility in the area of personnel management
    C. as precise as possible and practicable in the area of personnel management, but should allow considerable flexibility in the areas of function
    D. in general terms so as to allow considerable flexibility both in the areas of function and in the areas of personnel management

42. The LEAST important of the following reasons why a particular activity should be assigned to a unit which performs activities dissimilar to it is that

    A. close coordination is needed between the particular activity and other activities performed by the unit
    B. it will enhance the reputation and prestige of the unit supervisor
    C. the unit makes frequent use of the results of this particular activity
    D. the unit supervisor has a sound knowledge and understanding of the particular activity

43. A supervisor is put in charge of a special unit. She is exceptionally well-qualified for this assignment by her training and experience. One of her very close personal friends has been working for some time as a social investigator in this unit. Both the supervisor and investigator are certain that the rest of the investigators in the unit, many of whom have been in the bureau for a long time, know of this close relationship.
    Under these circumstances, the MOST advisable action for the supervisor to take is to

A. ask that either she be allowed to return to her old assignment or, if that cannot be arranged, that her friend be transferred to another unit in the center
B. avoid any overt sign of favoritism by acting impartially and with greater reserve when dealing with this investigator than with the rest of the staff
C. discontinue any socializing with this investigator either inside or outside the office so as to eliminate any gossip or dissatisfaction
D. not to review the situation with the investigator in order to arrive at a mutually acceptable plan of proper office decorum

44. In a conference on difficult cases between a recently appointed assistant supervisor and an experienced, above-average social investigator, the MOST valuable of the following services that the assistant supervisor can offer the investigator is a

A. detached point of view
B. knowledge of human needs
C. knowledge of the agency's basic rules and regulations
D. willingness to make decisions

45. Much attention has been focused of late in social welfare circles on ways of reaching and helping multi-problem families.
The one of the following approaches which is MOST important as an early step in working with these families is

A. contacts with educational, social, vocational, and religious services in the community to see what resources there might be for referral
B. referral to appropriate resources for medical or psychiatric care
C. the worker's taking active responsibility for determining its needs with the family and for helping them secure all of the needed discretionary services for which they are legally eligible
D. thorough determination of the causative factors responsible for the difficulties facing the family and the extent to which each member of the family has been responsible therefor

46. In helping young investigators in their work with aged clients, one of the MOST important, and often MOST difficult, principles to get across is the need

A. for knowledge of various community services for the aged, i.e., different kinds of placement facilities, recreational resources, etc.
B. to move more slowly with old people, e.g., to repeat explanations, etc.
C. to recognize that old people are different from each other and need to be individualized just as other clients do
D. to take more responsibility for planning with aged clients

47. The MOST important of the following reasons why the average resident of a deteriorated slum neighborhood resists relocation to an area in the suburbs with better physical accommodations is that he

A. does not recognize as undesirable the characteristics which are responsible for deterioration of the neighborhood
B. has some expectation of neighborly assistance in his old home in times of stress and adversity
C. hopes for better days when he may be able to become a figure of some importance and envy in the old neighborhood

D. is attuned to the noise of the city and fears the quiet of the suburbs

48. From a psychological and sociological point of view, the MOST important of the following dangers to the persons living in an economically depressed area in which the only step taken by governmental and private social agencies to assist these persons in the granting of a dole is that

    A. industry will be reluctant to expand its operations in that area
    B. the dole will encourage additional non-producers to enter the area
    C. the residents of the area will probably have to find their own solution to their problems
    D. their permanent dependency will be fostered

49. The term *real wages* is generally used by economists to mean the

    A. amount of take-home pay left after taxes, social security, and other such deductions have been made by the employer
    B. average wage actually earned during a calendar or fiscal year
    C. family income expressed on a per capita basis
    D. wages expressed in terms of its buying power

50. Most authorities in the field of special education believe that the BEST of the following actions to take in connection with the education of a blind child of pre-school age is to

    A. arrange to have the blind child educated in a home or nursery school setting with one sighted child on whom he can depend for help with his needs
    B. enroll the blind child in a nursery school with sighted children when he is ready for group experience
    C. have the blind child taught simple games and handicrafts at home in a sheltered setting apart from the pressure of group activity and competition with sighted children
    D. place the blind child in a residential school for the totally blind where he can become more comfortable and adjusted to his condition in the company of his blind peers

51. It has at times been suggested that an effective way to eradicate juvenile delinquency would be to arrest and punish the parents for the criminal actions of their delinquent children.
    The one of the following which is the CHIEF defect of this proposal is that

    A. it fails to get at the cause of the delinquent act and tends to further weaken disturbed parent-child relationships
    B. since the criminally inclined child has apparently demonstrated little love or affection for his parents, the child will be unlikely to amend his behavior in order to avoid hurting his parents
    C. the child who commits anti-social acts does so in most cases in order to hurt his parents so that this proposal would not only increase the parents' sorrow but would also serve as an incentive to more delinquency by the child
    D. the punishment should be limited to the person who commits the illegal action rather than to those who are most interested in his welfare

52. Surveys which have compared the relative stability of marriages between white persons with marriages between non-white persons in this country have shown that among blacks there is

   A. a significantly higher percentage of spouses absent from the household than among whites
   B. a significantly higher percentage of spouses absent from the household than among whites living in the South, but the opposite is true in the Northeast
   C. a significantly lower percentage of spouses absent from the household than among whites
   D. no significant difference in the percentages of spouses absent from the household when compared with the white population

53. A phenomenon found in the cultural and recreational patterns of European immigrant families in America is that, generally, the foreign-born adults

   A. as well as their children, tend to retain and continue their old-world activities and adopt the cultural and recreational customs of America
   B. as well as their children, tend to retain and continue their old-world cultural and recreational pursuits, finding it equally difficult to adopt those of America
   C. tend soon to drop their old pursuits and adopt the cultural and recreational patterns of America while their children find it somewhat more difficult to make this change
   D. tend to retain and continue their old-world cultural and recreational pursuits while their children tend to rapidly replace these by the games and cultural patterns of America

54. Certain mores of migrant groups are strengthened under the impact of their contact with the native society while other mores are weakened. In the case of Puerto Ricans who have come to New York City, the effect of such contact upon their traditional family structure has been a _____ of the former _____ family structure.

   A. *strengthening; maternalistic*
   B. *strengthening; paternalistic*
   C. *weakening; maternalistic*
   D. *weakening; paternalistic*

55. Administrative reviews and special studies by independent experts, as reported by the present Secretary of Health, Education and Welfare, indicate that the proportion of recipients of public assistance who receive such assistance through willful misrepresentation of the facts is

   A. less than 1%   B. about 4%
   C. between 4% and 7%   D. between 7% and 10%

Questions 56-60.

DIRECTIONS: Answer Questions 56 through 60 SOLELY on the basis of the following three charts concerning referrals made by the Department of Welfare of the City of Millville.

TABLE 1. REFERRALS MADE FOR SPECIALIZED HELP

	Number of Referrals For			
Year	Psychiatric Help	Alcoholism	Vocational Rehabilitation	Homemaking Service
2003	110	60	180	20
2004	120	36	205	36
2005	80	25	275	40
2006	90	16	250	40
2007	100	5	230	38

TABLE 2. RESULTS OF REFERRALS FOR VOCATIONAL REHABILITATION

Year	Total Referrals	Appeared For Initial Interviews	Kept Appointments, Cooperative	Treatment Successful	Off Welfare As Result Of Treatment
2003	180	120	40	30	25
2004	205	180	120	80	60
2005	275	220	160	120	100
2006	250	215	160	130	105
2007	230	220	170	128	90

TABLE 3.
Average Percentage of "Budget for Specialized Help" Expended on Each Category for the five-year period 2003-07.

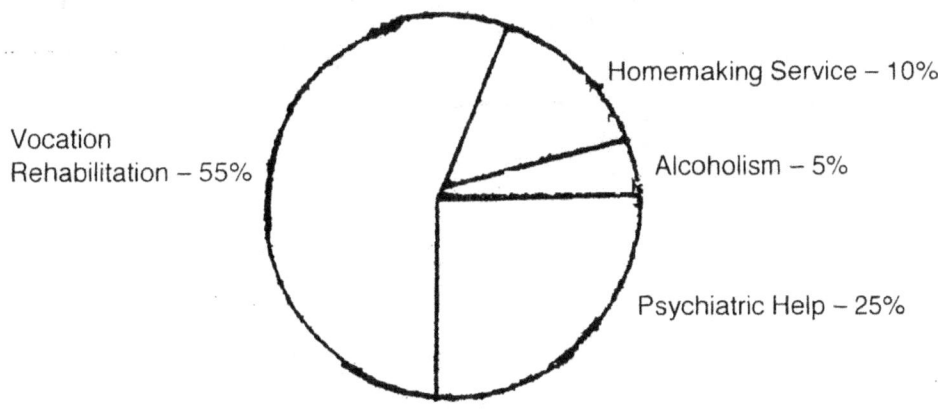

Vocation Rehabilitation – 55%
Homemaking Service – 10%
Alcoholism – 5%
Psychiatric Help – 25%

56. Of the following, the two years when an equal percentage of clients who were cooperative when referred for vocational rehabilitation were successfully treated were

    A. 2003 and 2004
    B. 2003 and 2005
    C. 2004 and 2006
    D. 2005 and 2006
    E. 2006 and 2007

16 (#1)

57. If, in 2006, the number of referrals had been increased for alcoholism by 10, for vocational rehabilitation by 40, and for homemaking services by 5, then the total number of referrals for specialized help that year would have increased by MOST NEARLY

    A. 1.5%   B. 7%   C. 14%   D. 30%   E. 55%

57.___

58. Although there are actually no errors in the charts given above, suppose that one of the following figures was recorded incorrectly and constituted the one and only error in the charts.
By carefully inspecting the charts, one could always tell that there was an error if the error was made in the figure for the

    A. average percentage utilization for psychiatric help of the "Budget for Specialized Help" from 2003 through 2007
    B. number of referrals for alcoholism in 2007
    C. number of referrals for vocational rehabilitation who were removed from welfare as a result of treatment in 2005
    D. number referred for vocational rehabilitation in 2006 who appeared for initial interview

58.___

59. In 2005, the budget for specialized help was $200,000, and the amount expended for vocational rehabilitation was $8,000 more than the amount represented by the average percentage expended for vocational rehabilitation for the period 2003 through 2007. The amount expended for vocational rehabilitation in 2005 was MOST NEARLY

    A. $4,400   B. $19,000   C. $44,000   D. $110,000   E. $118,000

59.___

60. Assume that the average size of the budget for specialized help for the five-year period 2003 through 2007 was $360,000 per year.
The average cost per referral for psychiatric help during this period was MOST NEARLY

    A. $180   B. $360   C. $720   D. $900
    E. cannot be determined from the data given

60.___

KEY (CORRECT ANSWERS)

1.	D	16.	C	31.	B	46.	C
2.	C	17.	A	32.	D	47.	B
3.	D	18.	B	33.	C	48.	D
4.	A	19.	D	34.	A	49.	D
5.	C	20.	D	35.	C	50.	B
6.	B	21.	B	36.	A	51.	A
7.	B	22.	C	37.	B	52.	A
8.	D	23.	A	38.	C	53.	D
9.	C	24.	A	39.	B	54.	D
10.	D	25.	B	40.	D	55.	A
11.	D	26.	D	41.	A	56.	B
12.	C	27.	A	42.	B	57.	C
13.	D	28.	B	43.	A	58.	D
14.	A	29.	B	44.	A	59.	E
15.	B	30.	C	45.	C	60.	D

EXAMINATION SECTION
TEST 1

DIRECTIONS: Each question or incomplete statement is followed by several suggested answers or completions. Select the one that BEST answers the question or completes the statement. *PRINT THE LETTER OF THE CORRECT ANSWER IN THE SPACE AT THE RIGHT.*

1. Recently, the State Department of Labor declared that *city employers are faced with a developing manpower shortage which will grow worse if business continues at high levels.* Since public welfare agencies have a special responsibility for preserving the self-maintenance capacities of physically handicapped persons, it is appropriate that during periods of increased employment such as that illustrated above, the Department of Welfare should place its GREATEST emphasis on

    A. developing special placement opportunities for all disabled persons
    B. providing vocational training for newly opened job opportunities
    C. recognizing that the disabled can never become as self-maintaining as the physically fit and will, therefore, continue to need assistance
    D. directing the disabled to those occupations related to the special senses which the disabled often develop
    E. facilitating the efforts of the disabled to obtain employment, whether temporary or permanent, partial or total

1.____

2. In order to meet more adequately the public assistance needs occasioned by sudden changes in the national economy, welfare agencies in general recommend, as a matter of preference, that

    A. each locality build up reserve funds to care for needy unemployed persons in order to avoid a breakdown of local resources such as occurred during the Depression
    B. the federal government assume total responsibility for the administration of public assistance
    C. state settlement laws be strictly enforced so that unemployed workers will be encouraged to move from the emergency industry centers to their former homes
    D. a federal-state-local program of general assistance be established with need as the only eligibility requirement
    E. eligibility requirements be tightened to assure that only legitimately worthy local residents receive the available assistance

2.____

3. The MOST practical method of maintaining income for the majority of aged persons who are no longer able to work, or for the families of those workers who are deceased, is

    A. a comprehensive system of non-categorical assistance on a basis of cash payments
    B. an integrated system of public assistance and extensive work relief programs
    C. a coordinated system of providing care in institutions and foster homes
    D. a system of contributory insurance in which a cash benefit is paid as a matter of right
    E. an expanded system of diagnostic and treatment centers

3.____

4. With the establishment of insurance and assistance programs under the Social Security Act, many institutional programs for the aged have tended to the greatest extent toward an increased emphasis on providing, of the following types of assistance,

   A. care for the aged by denominational groups
   B. care for children requiring institutional treatment
   C. recreational facilities for the able-bodied aged
   D. training facilities in industrial homework for the aged
   E. care for the chronically ill and infirm aged

4.____

5. According to studies made by the Federal Security Agency, the benefits received by beneficiaries of the old age and survivors insurance program during past years

   A. were too small to be basically helpful
   B. represented about a third of the resources of most beneficiaries
   C. were an unimportant factor in income maintenance
   D. constituted the major portion of the family's income
   E. constituted about one-quarter of the average public assistance grant

5.____

6. Of the following terms, the one which BEST describes the Social Security Act is

   A. enabling legislation   B. regulatory statute
   C. appropriations act   D. act of mandamus
   E. provisional enactment

6.____

7. Of the following, the term which MOST accurately describes an *appropriation* is

   A. authority to spend   B. itemized estimate
   C. *fund* accounting   D. anticipated expenditure
   E. executive budget

7.____

8. When business expansion causes a demand for labor, the worker group which benefits MOST immediately is the group comprising

   A. employed workers
   B. inexperienced workers under 21 years of age
   C. experienced workers 21 to 25 years of age
   D. inexperienced older workers
   E. experienced workers over 40 years of age

8.____

9. The MOST important failure in our present system of providing social work services in local communities is the

   A. absence of adequate facilities for treating mental illness
   B. lack of coordination of available data and service in the community
   C. poor quality of the casework services provided by the public agencies
   D. limitations of the probation and parole services
   E. inadequacy of private family welfare services

9.____

10. It is generally considered advisable for a public assistance agency to make special allowances for the purchase of physical appliances for its recipients only when the

    A. desired appliance has been prescribed by a physician and when the client is physically, mentally, and emotionally able to use it
    B. agency has a special fund to meet such additional expenditures

10.____

C. fact is verified that employment will be available if the client uses the appliance
D. purchase will assure the individual of becoming self-maintaining again
E. desired appliance has been prescribed by a social worker as necessary to compensate the client for loss of a normal bodily function

11. Recent studies of the relationship between incidence of illness and the use of available treatment services among various population groups in the United States show that

    A. while lower-income families use medical services with greater frequency, total expenditures are greater among the upper-income group
    B. although the average duration of a period of medical care increases with increasing income, the average frequency of obtaining care decreases with increasing income
    C. adequacy of medical service is inversely related to frequency of illness and size of family income
    D. families in the higher-income brackets have a heavier incidence of illness and make greater use of medical service than do those in the lower-income brackets
    E. both as to frequency and duration, the distribution of illness falls equally on all groups, but the use of medical service increases with income

12. The category of disease which most public health departments and authorities usually are NOT equipped to handle directly is that of

    A. chronic disease
    B. bronchial disturbances
    C. venereal disease
    D. mosquito-borne diseases
    E. incipient forms of tuberculosis

13. Recent statistical analyses of the causes of death in the United States indicate that medical science has now reached the stage where it would be preferable to increase its research toward control, among the following, PRINCIPALLY of

    A. accidents   B. suicides
    C. communicable diseases D. chronic disease
    E. infant mortality

14. Although the distinction between mental disease and mental deficiency is fairly definite, both these conditions USUALLY represent

    A. diseases of one part or organ of the body rather than of the whole person
    B. an inadequacy existing from birth or shortly afterwards, and appearing as a simplicity of intelligence
    C. a deficiency developing later in life and characterized by distortions of attitude and belief
    D. inadequacies in meeting life situations and in conducting one's affairs
    E. somewhat transitory conditions characterized by disturbances of consciousness

15. According to studies made by reliable medical research organizations in the United States, differences among the states in proportion of physicians to population are MOST directly related to the

    A. geographic resources among the states
    B. skill of the physicians

C. relative proportions of urban and rural people in the population of the states
D. number of specialists in the ranks of the physicians
E. health status of the people in the various states

16. MOST of the mentally ill who are hospitalized for long periods of time are in institutions administered by

    A. the U.S. Public Health Service
    B. county and municipal government
    C. the Veterans Administration
    D. the state government
    E. psychiatrists in private practice

17. In the development and maintenance of a social group work program, it is accepted that certain principles must be recognized if the program is to achieve maximum value. Of the following, the one consideration which would be INAPPROPRIATE as a base on which to set the planning and operation of such a program is that it should

    A. be individualized and designed to meet specific needs
    B. develop out of interests and needs of group members
    C. be planned, conducted, and evaluated by the group
    D. involve the group worker as a helping person
    E. develop from a series of initial and follow-up surveys conducted by trained personnel

18. One of the MAIN advantages of incorporating a charitable organization is that

    A. gifts or property of a corporation cannot be held in perpetuity
    B. gifts to unincorporated charitable organizations are not deductible from the taxable income
    C. incorporation gives less legal standing or *personality* than an informal partnership
    D. members of a corporation cannot be held liable for debts contracted by the organization
    E. a corporate organization cannot be sued

19. In conjunction with court and educational authorities, the Division of Physically Handicapped Children administers a program of care for persons under 2-1 years of age who, by reason of physical defect or infirmity, are totally or partially incapacitated for education or occupation. All of the following types of care are provided by this division EXCEPT

    A. surgical treatment
    B. medical treatment
    C. therapeutic treatment
    D. furnishing of prosthetic appliances or devices
    E. procuring scholarships for summer camps

20. If a client is to receive continuing services or assistance from the Department of Welfare requests help in which the Department has an interest and which it cannot provide, but which can be furnished by another agency in the community, the worker should USUALLY

A. interpret the other agency's function to the client and determine how best to use its services, thus conserving the client's time and preventing possible embarrassment to him
B. forego discussion of the other agency's services with the client, since it is confusing for two welfare agencies to attempt to serve the same client at the same time
C. send a case summary to the other agency and request that a worker from that agency call at the client's home to assist in the working out of his problem
D. not suggest the agency to which the client can apply and ask him to return and discuss the plans developed with the other agency
E. not advise the client that his situation will be discussed with another agency in the community and that he will be notified whether the agency can accept his case and be of service to him

21. It is important to use a skilled worker to conduct the initial interview with an applicant for assistance in the Department of Welfare CHIEFLY because

    A. inaccurate information concerning eligibility requirements and the documentary evidence which must be produced may then be checked expeditiously
    B. whenever possible, the assistance plan should be developed during the course of the first interview
    C. only a highly skilled worker can make a satisfactory investigation of the applicant's eligibility
    D. the relationship established between worker and applicant during this interview usually determines the departmental policies affecting the case
    E. the effectiveness of the Department's subsequent work with the client is often influenced materially by the kind of relationship established in this first contact

22. During an interview, a client may seem overwhelmed by the amount of data needed by the Department of Welfare in order to establish his eligibility, although most of the required information, as a rule, is easily obtained.
    The one of the following responses by the intake interviewer which could be expected to reassure such a client BEST is

    A. "All this information is very important and you should try your best to get it as soon as possible"
    B. "If you think you'll have trouble getting this material together, I'll do it for you"
    C. "It sounds like a lot, but it is actually very simple; without realizing it, you probably have most of the material on hand already"
    D. "There's no need to be overwhelmed by the amount of this material; all our clients have to get it together"
    E. "Oh, I'm sure you can do it"

23. Of the following objectives, the one which an initial interview with an applicant for public assistance is usually designed to serve is to

    A. afford the client an opportunity to express his needs and desires
    B. allow the worker time to secure all the information he wants
    C. condition the direction of service
    D. record verbatim the client's statement regarding need
    E. include a discussion of the client's family and other personal relationships

24. A MOST appropriate condition in the use of direct questions to obtain personal data in an interview is that, whenever possible,

   A. the direct questions be used only as a means of encouraging the person interviewed to talk about himself
   B. provision be made for recording the information
   C. the direct questions be used only after all other methods have failed
   D. the person being interviewed understand the reason for requesting the information
   E. the direct questions be used only at the start of the interview

25. Suppose that a social investigator, during his initial interview with a client, notices that the client is becoming antagonistic for no apparent reason.
   In this situation, the investigator should USUALLY

   A. explain to the client that unwarranted antagonism is really due to factors deeply hidden in the client's own personality
   B. terminate the interview with a statement to the effect that the client should return for another interview when he feels more kindly disposed toward the interviewer
   C. make clear in his actions that there is no retaliatory disapproval and continue to try to understand the client's difficulties
   D. admit to the client that he is aware of the existing antagonism and that he is unable to find the reason for it
   E. ask the client why he feels antagonistic toward him since he himself has not given him any grounds for such a reaction

26. When a client informs the social investigator of a plan to move permanently to another state, it is the responsibility of the investigator to advise the client that

   A. he should apply for continued approval of his grant on the basis of *temporary absence* since his plan for permanent removal may not materialize
   B. the last check he receives before leaving the city should be used for necessary transportation and expenses while traveling to his new abode
   C. he will be ineligible for any continued assistance from the Department of Welfare and that eligibility in the new community will depend upon local requirements
   D. he should not move to a new state since the assistance in that state will probably not be adequate for his needs
   E. the Department of Welfare will arrange to have the public assistance agency in the community to which he is going make an immediate investigation in order that the continuance of his public assistance grant will not be interrupted

27. Suppose that the mother of a family receiving public assistance is recovering from an operation at home and that her doctor reports she will be unable to care for her children for one month.
   In such a situation, it would be MOST appropriate for the social investigator to

   A. recommend the assignment of a Department of Welfare homemaker in accordance with the doctor's report
   B. refer the children to a temporary shelter
   C. visit the neighborhood to find a free home for the children
   D. recommend that foster care be provided
   E. write to legally responsible relatives living in an adjacent state to explore the possibility of their providing care for the children

28. In computing the budget for a family applying for public assistance where there is a lodger living in the household, Department of Welfare policy requires that the social investigator should deduct the

   A. total income received from the lodger from the total estimate of the family's needs
   B. total income from the lodger minus the cost of food for any meals provided from the total estimate of the family's needs
   C. total income from the lodger minus an adjusted allowance for fuel and lighting
   D. net income from the total estimate of the family's needs
   E. total income received from the lodger minus the proportionate cost of room rental

29. Experiences with respect to use of cash payments to public assistance clients have established that, basically, this form of assistance is more satisfactory than any other type because cash payments

   A. are less destructive of the client's self-respect than relief in kind
   B. are less likely to call for bookkeeping skill than payments by requisition
   C. are cheaper to administer than other forms of assistance
   D. are more acceptable to commercial concerns than order slips
   E. make possible larger grants to clients than other forms of assistance

Questions 30-39.

DIRECTIONS: Levels of approval for certain types of allowances are set forth in the Department of Welfare manual, POLICIES GOVERNING THE ADMINISTRATION OF PUBLIC ASSISTANCE. In Questions 30 through 39 below are listed certain types of allowances for which approval is necessary according to departmental policy. Answer each of these questions in the following manner:

ANSWER IF THE TYPE OF ALLOWANCE REQUIRES APPROVAL OF
   A. - the unit supervisor only
   B. - the case supervisor in addition to the unit supervisor
   C. - case consultation, in addition to unit and case supervisors
   D. - case consultation and the resource division, in addition to unit and case supervisors
   E. - the resource division, in addition to unit and case supervisors

30. Bond and mortgage waiver, after refusal to execute.

31. Carfare to attend a special school for the blind and deaf.

32. Conditional sale and mortgage on personal property.

33. Emergency assistance, first recurring or non-recurring agent.

34. Repair allowance for a homeowner.

35. Housing project security deposit.

36. Guide fees for blind persons.

37. Rent arrears, including costs and fees.

38. Special diet, upon medical recommendation.

39. Referral of a homeless man to a municipal shelter.

40. Coordination of staff activity in a large agency can usually be effected MOST successfully by an executive through the use of

   A. written reports
   B. face-to-face contact in meetings with department heads
   C. observation of performance
   D. permanent assignment of staff to specific functions
   E. procedural instructions

41. Organization charts and manuals are essential to the sound administration of a public welfare agency.
    In this respect, the MOST important purpose of a manual in the Department of Welfare is to serve as a

   A. means of preventing duplication
   B. device for eliminating community misinterpretation of the Department's activities
   C. tool for achieving orderly operations
   D. method of maintaining executive controls
   E. system of compiling case decisions

42. Failure on the part of a caseworker in a public assistance agency to recognize the close relationship between standards of performance with regard to office routine and standards of work with clients is, of the following, usually due to the fact that

   A. his supervisor has continued to assume responsibilities which the case worker should carry
   B. his supervisor has not made clear to the case worker each aspect of the job or of the total responsibilities of the worker
   C. the case worker should not be the person who is required to prepare reports
   D. the case worker's primary function is the treatment of social problems
   E. the clerical staff has not adequately performed those of its duties related to the work of the case worker

43. In helping a social investigator deal with a case in which the client is harassed by a difficult family situation, the supervisor usually can be of GREATEST assistance by

   A. showing the investigator that his own family experiences parallel those of the client
   B. helping the investigator balance the interests of all members of the family
   C. advising the investigator that family matters are frequently too personal to be discussed in detail
   D. suggesting that a psychiatrist be brought in on the case
   E. teaching the investigator how to discover which member of the family is most maladjusted

44. Initial interviews with applicants for public assistance require a high degree of skill on the part of the interviewer PRIMARILY because

    A. applicants are usually uncertain as to what kind of factual information will aid their cause
    B. applicants who have had no previous experience with social agencies usually are overwhelmed by the newness of the experience
    C. the feeling of economic dependency is usually emotionally disturbing to the applicant
    D. applicants are naturally suspicious of any agency that administers public funds
    E. the worker and the applicant are strangers to one another and each is uncertain as to how the other will interpret his remarks

45. During a case conference, if a unit supervisor repeatedly returns to a statement of points already made, the case supervisor should USUALLY

    A. discuss some neutral subject until the unit supervisor is more composed
    B. insert a question leading to a different topic altogether
    C. terminate the conference as soon as possible in order not to waste time
    D. attempt to direct the flow of discussion by expressing his own opinion on the subject
    E. let the unit supervisor talk himself out on this topic

46. With respect to case recording, the Department of Welfare has developed a new type of streamlined case record which will contain all the essential factors pertinent to current eligibility and which can be maintained in a usable and readable condition on a continuing basis. The development of this plan was based on a consideration of the essential attributes of good recording in a public assistance agency. Of the following, the one which is NOT in accord with the above-mentioned plan is

    A. accuracy in recording, which reflects the point of view of the client and of the social investigator
    B. elimination of all information except the documentation of eligibility based on points of statutory evidence
    C. freedom from bias or prejudice in order that the client may receive the full service due to him
    D. brevity and conciseness, which make the record more serviceable for review by the social investigator and by his supervisors
    E. clarity, which is obtained largely by adherence to common rules of rhetoric and which provides coherence and unity

47. When Children's Placement Services refers an undercare case to a welfare center for public assistance, the social investigator to whom the case is assigned should

    A. review the investigation made by Children's Placement Services and supplement it with whatever information is necessary
    B. accept the case as referred for the appropriate type of public assistance
    C. make a complete investigation of all factors of eligibility in the same manner as for any other applicant for public assistance
    D. talk to the client and make a referral to a private agency
    E. make an immediate referral of the client to an available job in order to prevent dependency

48. Under certain circumstances, a court order imposes responsibility on the unmarried mother and the father for sharing the support of a child born out of wedlock. The court which has jurisdiction over such matters is the

    A. Supreme Court
    B. Children's Court
    C. Magistrates' Court
    D. Domestic Relations Court
    E. Court of Special Sessions

49. Social workers who work principally with maladjusted children find that the children's problems MOST frequently originate in

    A. health factors
    B. religious attitudes
    C. teachers' attitudes
    D. parental attitudes
    E. economic conditions

50. Persistent feeding difficulties in children are MOST often related to

    A. poverty in the home
    B. basic personality maladjustments
    C. high intelligence
    D. the presence of other children in the room
    E. the number of older and younger children in the family

51. If a person attempts to conceal his inadequacies in certain activities by overindulging in some other activity, he is MOST liable to do so because he

    A. is compensating for his inadequacies
    B. has a delusion that he is inadequate in some activities
    C. has rationalized that the skill in the latter activity is more easily developed
    D. is trying to develop skill in the former activities by indulging in the latter
    E. is projecting the pleasure he finds in the former activities to the latter

52. The casework concept of *acceptable,* when applied to behavior that deviates from what society expects, implies

    A. refusing to pass judgment on the behavior of others
    B. accepting all behavior without attempting to evaluate it
    C. condoning behavior which the client seems incapable of changing
    D. exercising non-judgmental impartiality
    E. active understanding of the underlying feelings rather than of the behavior itself

53. When a prospective employer requests that a person of a particular race, color, or religion be sent to him in order to fill a job opening in a department store, the employment interviewer should IMMEDIATELY

    A. report the employer to the State Commission Against Discrimination
    B. advise the employer that he is violating the law and that if he does not accept an able and available person, he will be reported to the State Commission Against Discrimination
    C. remove the employer's name as a source of employment referrals and notify Central Office so that other welfare centers may be informed of the situation
    D. arrange to interview the employer in order to determine whether there are valid reasons for his request
    E. make an employment referral if a public assistance recipient who meets the specifications of the employer is available

54. The early English Poor Laws influenced American administration of relief in their emphasis upon the

    A. giving of adequate assistance
    B. centralization of relief administration under a national authority
    C. local character of administration and financing
    D. failure to enforce the responsibility of relatives for their needy kin
    E. discrimination made in providing for the care and treatment of clients on the basis of their individual needs

55. The undifferentiated treatment of clients given by public welfare services in the eighteenth and nineteenth centuries was due not only to the state of social and economic development but also to the

    A. limitations imposed by the lack of adequate institutional facilities
    B. prevalence of religious condemnation of social inadequacy
    C. absence of technical knowledge necessary for social diagnosis
    D. homogeneous nature of the social structure itself
    E. relative isolation of individual communities

KEY (CORRECT ANSWERS)

1. E	16. D	31. A	46. B
2. D	17. E	32. C	47. A
3. D	18. D	33. A	48. E
4. E	19. E	34. E	49. D
5. D	20. A	35. A	50. B
6. A	21. E	36. B	51. A
7. A	22. C	37. B	52. D
8. B	23. A	38. A	53. B
9. B	24. D	39. A	54. C
10. A	25. C	40. B	55. C
11. C	26. C	41. C	
12. A	27. A	42. B	
13. D	28. A	43. B	
14. D	29. A	44. C	
15. C	30. D	45. B	

EXAMINATION SECTION
TEST 1

DIRECTIONS: Each question or incomplete statement is followed by several suggested answers or completions. Select the one that BEST answers the question or completes the statement. *PRINT THE LETTER OF THE CORRECT ANSWER IN THE SPACE AT THE RIGHT.*

1. Because of public reaction incident to an announcement of revised public assistance allowances, the members of your staff express concern over how to justify the position of the department.
   As a supervisor, you should inform your staff that the revised allowances represent a _____ allowance to meet essential needs.

   A. new policy based on furnishing a minimum
   B. new policy based on furnishing a minimum but adequate
   C. continuing policy based on furnishing a minimum
   D. continuing policy based on furnishing a minimum but adequate

2. Good public relations are essential to the sucess of a public welfare agency's program. Of the following means of maintaining good public relations, the MOST important for the public welfare agency is

   A. the development of a cooperative, interested attitude on the part of the *press*
   B. the education of the community as a whole by the regular release of informative but lively human interest stories
   C. concern for the welfare of the clients and prompt and efficient methods of meeting need
   D. the development of good relationships with the other social agencies in the community to insure their support of the agency's program

3. Although human relations have large significance in the job of the supervisor in the Department of Welfare, it is NOT necessarily true that the

   A. supervisor must be a leader in order to do his job well
   B. supervisor must be able to tell his staff how to do their jobs in the right way
   C. supervisor is part of the management of the Department of Welfare
   D. ability to get along with people is the sole stock in trade of the supervisor

4. Management is the art and science of preparing, organizing, and directing human effort applied to control the forces and utilize the materials of nature for the benefit of man. From the point of view of an employee in the Department of Welfare, this statement means that when he is promoted to the position of supervisor,

   A. he will be working directly with the raw materials of the social service field in dealing with clients
   B. he will no longer be concerned so much with *human relations* as when he dealt with clients directly in the capacity of social investigator
   C. his efforts from then on should be directed toward doing things himself
   D. his efforts from then on should be directed toward getting others to do things

5. Office organization charts, if they are to be used as aids to proper supervision of Welfare Department personnel, should be

   A. used as originally drawn up so that the type of organization function can be easily memorized by the entire staff
   B. revised constantly because office organizations are constantly undergoing change
   C. eliminated entirely and developed in some new form since no organization chart is an accurate representation of actual working conditions
   D. checked against actual working conditions in order to present a current and accurate state of affairs

6. A sustained relationship between supervisor and subordinate staff is necessary because the

   A. department must avoid needless expenditure of public funds
   B. worker learns to relate himself helpfully to clients as he learns to take help from the supervisor
   C. worker must have some source from which to get answers to his problems
   D. case problems in public assistance require a degree of skill that social investigators do not have themselves

7. Looking at the job of the supervisor in the Department of Welfare in terms of production or accomplishment, one may BEST say that, of the following, the *tools* with which the supervisor does his work are

   A. rules and regulations	B. records and orders
   C. office equipment	D. people

8. The supervisor carries out his responsibility for maintaining the department's standards of case work practice by

   A. delegating responsibility for the case load to the assistant supervisors and social investigators and reviewing and passing on their work in each case
   B. delegating responsibility for the case load to the assistant supervisors and social investigators and directing their activities in relation to each case
   C. establishing and using controls necessary to keep aware of case load activity and interviewing where there is indication of breakdown in the standards of practice
   D. individual development through supervisory conferences and training meetings

9. A supervisor is transferred to a new district office. In a group conference with his staff on the first day, he should

   A. discuss with them their ways of relating to the previous supervisor and tell them that, for the present, he will fit into the established schedule
   B. tell them about himself, his ways of working, what he expects of his staff, and the methods of supervision he intends to follow
   C. learn as much as possible about each member of the staff so that he can get down to a constructive relationship with them as soon as possible
   D. conduct only a brief introductory meeting in a friendly manner without reference to the work situation

10. It is the conception of the Department of Welfare that the plan to distribute checks semi-monthly to families approved for public assistance

    A. represents an entirely new experiment in the methods of distributing relief allowances
    B. is required by law since relief allowances must be received in advance
    C. will make management easier for relief recipients
    D. must be adopted even against its better judgment because of recommendations made by the Federal Security Agency

11. The degree of success or failure which can be achieved with applications of the official service rating system now in use depends MAINLY on the

    A. immediate supervisor of the employee being rated
    B. the Municipal Civil Service Commission
    C. the employee being rated
    D. the central office of the Department of Welfare

12. The step-by-step process of training a subordinate by instruction, regardless of what is to be taught, is

    A. preparation of the learner, presentation of instruction matter, performance tryout, follow-up
    B. presentation of instruction matter, performance try-out, preparation of learner, follow-up
    C. performance tryout, follow-up, preparation of the learner, presentation of instruction matter
    D. presentation of instruction matter, performance tryout, follow-up

13. Supervisors in the Department of Welfare should caution staff personnel to avoid over-willingness to do things for the client because

    A. they are not charged with any responsibility toward the client
    B. all possible resources must be exhausted before anyone may become a recipient of public assistance
    C. this approach to the client may foster dependency
    D. eligibility is established by the written record, and the personal factor does not enter into it

14. A unit supervisor on your staff reports that one of the recipients of public assistance in his case load is a war veteran who held National Service Life Insurance during the Gulf War for a period of ten months, but who has done nothing to collect his share of the dividend.
    You should advise this unit head that

    A. the veteran cannot receive any dividend since he held the insurance less than one year
    B. the veteran should apply for the dividend since any funds received as a result of such payments must be budgeted as a resource
    C. the veteran should apply for the dividend since these funds are legally exempt from any use except in the manner to be determined by the recipient
    D. whether the veteran wishes to apply for the dividend is subject to his own wishes and not within the purview of the Department of Welfare

4 (#1)

15. A CORRECT evaluation by the supervisor of the conference method as compared with parliamentary procedure would be that the group conference

   A. inhibits the expression of free opinion
   B. dispenses with the technicalities of formal debate
   C. is slow and awkward when considered in terms of requirements of the work of the Department of Welfare
   D. makes for easier control of the situation by the person in charge of the meeting

16. Faced with the alternative of conducting a conference or giving a lecture to a group of associates in the Department of Welfare, your decision in favor of the lecture would be justified only if

   A. your mental equipment is superior to that of the group
   B. you wish to make sure that every member of the group gains something from the meeting
   C. the time element is of some importance
   D. the subject to be considered is beyond the experience and knowledge of the group

17. The group conference as distinguished from the individual conference as a method of staff development can be used BEST when

   A. the material to be covered is informational
   B. it might be difficult to handle individual reactions to the material of the meeting
   C. there is a training need that is more or less common to the group
   D. the group is not too divergent in background and level of development

18. Good supervision is selective because

   A. it is not necessary to direct all the activities of the person
   B. a supervisor would never have time to know the whole case load of a worker
   C. workers resent too much help from a supervisor
   D. too much case reading is a waste of valuable time

19. In developing the supervisory relationship with an assistant supervisor, a supervisor should aim to

   A. give the assistant supervisor a feeling of strength on which he can depend for case decisions
   B. give the assistant supervisor a feeling of security so that he can be flexible in his application of policy and procedure when necessary
   C. be as cooperative as possible so that the assistant supervisor will be cooperative with his staff in return
   D. be as interested as possible in the assistant supervisor's personal problems which he feels are affecting his work

20. At the end of his probationary period, a supervisor should be considered potentially valuable in his position if he shows

   A. awareness of his areas of strength and weakness, identification with the administration of the department, and ability to learn under supervision
   B. skill in case work, supervision, and administration, and a friendly, democratic approach to the staff

C. knowledge of departmental policies and procedures and ability to carry them out, ability to use authority, and ability to direct the work of the staff
D. an identification with the department, acceptance of responsibility, and ability to give help to the individuals who are to be supervised

21. Suppose that during the first two months of your assignment as supervisor in the Department of Welfare, you receive numerous suggestions from the staff for the improvement of working conditions, production, etc.
You should

   A. inform the administrator that the large number of suggestions submitted must be evidence that something is seriously amiss in the management of the office
   B. ignore the suggestions for the time being since you are not sufficiently acquainted with your new assignment
   C. inform the staff that, in due time, every suggestion will receive your attention and such action as the facts may warrant
   D. call a brief meeting and explain that it would be inadvisable for you to take any action until you have at least completed your probationary period

22. After two months in a district office, you have an assistant supervisor who rarely comes to you for help, presents no cases for discussion at conferences, and discusses no problems of administration or personnel in his unit. He is friendly toward you in manner and accepts any suggestions you make, but seeks nothing from you.
As supervisor, you should

   A. select a random sampling of cases from his unit for review, review his unit controls, show him everything is not as fine as he imagined, and point out where he needs help
   B. discuss his transfer to another office with your administrator since there is apparently a personality clash between you
   C. continue the relationship as currently established, using every opportunity that presents itself to waken his interest in learning, to challenge his capacities, and to show him where you may have something to offer him
   D. draw up an evaluation in which you outline his strengths and weaknesses, and discuss this with him, particularly his failure to utilize supervision

23. Occasional participation of assistant supervisors and social investigators on committees formulating new procedures would be in line with good supervisory practice because

   A. they are the only ones who know from experience how present procedures are working out
   B. they thereby acquire an understanding of the difficulties to be overcome in getting agreement in the central office
   C. assistant supervisors and social investigators throughout the department will have a greater tendency to accept changes if their own groups have participated in the preliminary thinking
   D. all the assistant supervisors and social investigators will be better prepared to accept the changes because the committee members shared developments with them

24. In planning for the vacation period of an assistant supervisor, the BEST course of action for the supervisor to follow is to

   A. take responsibility for supervision of the unit himself as this will give him an opportunity to get to know the staff, to renew his skills in supervision of workers, and to evaluate the assistant supervisor from the knowledge of the unit so gained
   B. let the more responsible and capable workers take turns at the desk for one day each week to give them an opportunity to supervise and to show them that the supervisor is democratic in his relations with the staff
   C. leave the unit uncovered because workers should be able to function independently for a few weeks as long as the unit clerk can keep administrative controls going
   D. arrange for two other supervisors to divide the work of the unit and add to their normal responsibilities the supervision of staff and management of the unit for the period

25. An assistant supervisor complains to you about one of his workers who turns every conference into a battle by arguing every point made.
As supervisor, you should

   A. help the supervisor work out techniques of conference direction that will avoid his presentation of an opinion against which the worker can argue
   B. help the supervisor relate this behavior to the total knowledge about the worker to see whether a personality difficulty is involved
   C. arrange for a transfer of either worker or supervisor because obviously the latter is too new to handle such a difficult situation
   D. tell him to threaten to charge the worker with insubordination if he does not desist and come to conference in a more receptive mood for learning

26. An assistant supervisor has been in your office about a month. In her relations with staff, management of the unit, and conference with you, she seems to be making at least average adjustment and progress. In your group meetings, however, she contributes nothing to the discussion, raises no questions, takes occasional notes.
As supervisor, you should

   A. call on her for opinion or comment several times at each meeting until she gets accustomed to talking
   B. discuss her conduct directly with her at conference, finding out the source of the difficulty and working out an adjustment
   C. review her personnel folder to see if it throws a light on the problem and direct the content of the next group conference to an aspect of the job in which you know she is particularly interested
   D. recognize that some people are naturally reticent in large groups, and if her contribution in general to the unit is good, do not become concerned about this at all

27. The intake supervisor in the district in which you are supervisor tells you that he has never been able to manage a scheduled, limited conference relationship because of the nature of his job. When he needs help on a case, it must be available immediately because the client is right in the office, and he never can be regular in attendance at a scheduled conference because his workers need him to be available to them at all times.
In this situation, you should

A. tell him that you cannot work in this hit-or-miss fashion, and he will have to conform as do the other supervisors
B. accept his explanation because it is a busy office and there are tremendous pressures in intake
C. excuse the intake supervisor from future conferences
D. tell him you will schedule future conferences with him to begin directly after his arrival and before starting on the day's routine activities

28. As supervisor, you are assigned a recently promoted assistant supervisor who has had five years of experience as an investigator but no professional training or other social work experience.
In your first regular conference with him, you should

    A. give him an opportunity to discuss how his previous experience will help him in this new assignment and how he thinks you can be of help to him
    B. share with him some of your thinking and philosophy about supervision and agency function and let him discuss his thinking with you so that you get to know each other and form the basis for a relationship
    C. make this conference a typical conference and begin immediately to consider the problems he has met in his first days in the unit
    D. ask him what use he wants to make of the supervisory conference and adapt the content and method to suit his wishes

29. An assistant supervisor comes to conference periods regularly and seems ready to discuss any cases or problems you, as supervisor, present, but in the two months you have been supervising him, he has never brought any cases for discussion or raised any problems. When asked, he always says everything in his unit is *fine*.
Of the following, the LEAST constructive approach would be to

    A. put it to him very directly that he was not making good use of supervision and that you expect him to participate equally with you in this process
    B. review how your relationship with him got started and how it has developed in order to understand the problem better
    C. discuss one aspect of his unit functioning in detail to see what he meant by *fine* and how well he understood the problem
    D. bring nothing to the next few conferences yourself so that the burden of the discussion will be thrown on him

30. While attending a unit conference as an observer at the invitation of another supervisor, you hear an assistant supervisor emphasize the value of thorough knowledge of procedures raised by his staff without looking up a single point in the manual.
Asked by the supervisor what you should do about such an assistant supervisor in one of your units, you should reply that

    A. such a situation would not occur in any of your units because your staff has been trained differently
    B. you would discuss methods of staff development at your next individual conference with such an assistant
    C. you would do nothing about this because the statement made by the assistant supervisor may be entirely correct
    D. you cannot answer because this problem affects his unit and not any of yours

8 (#1)

31. In developing good methods of recording, the BEST statement of principle to give staff as a guide is to

    A. record everything considered to be pertinent to understanding the needs of the client, his eligibility for assistance, his capacity and efforts in self-help, and the worker's services and relationship with him
    B. follow an outline of record that will tell him what to read and where to place each item
    C. eliminate everything that took place at the interview except those few facts affecting eligibility and need
    D. record everything exactly as it happened so that nothing will be left out that might be useful at some later date

32. Overwhelmed with the feeling of responsibility for nearly one thousand cases, a relatively new assistant supervisor seeks your help in the problem of case reading.
    As supervisor, you should

    A. reassure him that it would be neither necessary nor advisable for him to know the entire case load in order to function adequately
    B. tell him that as a new supervisor, he is not expected to know any of the cases
    C. ask him what his plan is and give him help and support in working it out
    D. suggest that he read blocks of cases from one worker at a time so that he will become familiar with each personality and their various methods of working

33. *Hostility toward a supervisor is an unavoidable concomitant of growth.*
    In teaching a new group of supervisors, lately promoted from the field, the supervisor sh

    A. point out the fallacy in this idea as being the result of poor supervision rather than any supervision
    B. prepare them to maintain an interest in and a supporting relationship with their workers even where they are showing intensive hostility
    C. recognize the presence of hostility and deal with it immediately so that it does not interfere with the relationship
    D. avoid opportunities for the development of hostility by being as democratic and friendly as possible

34. Of the adjustments that must be made in moving up from assistant supervisor to supervisor, the MOST important at the outset is to

    A. effect a change in the nature of the relationship already developed with the assistant supervisors in the office
    B. get hold of the outstanding reports and unfinished work in the district and complete these
    C. make a statistical analysis of the case load to see what the problems are in general
    D. develop a cooperative relationship with the other supervisors

35. The supervisor's responsibility for maintaining the standard of eligibility in the case load is BEST carried out by

    A. reading as many cases as possible until he has firsthand knowledge of what is being done in the case load

B. delegating this responsibility through the assistant supervisors to the workers and establishing qualitative and quantitative case load controls
C. a good in-service training program
D. teaching the staff in his charge the department's concept of its standard eligibility and helping them individually to approach this standard as the maximum level of their ability

36. In evaluating a new worker at the end of his probationary period, the supervisor should consider the BEST criteria to consist of

    A. knowledge of agency policy and procedure, skill in social study, skill in interviewing, ability to help clients more toward independent solution of problems
    B. identification with the purposes of the agency, interest in people, ability to meet his own needs and to assist others, ability in the learning role and beginnings of skill in social study and diagnosis
    C. identification with the agency, good administrative ability, interest in meeting other people's needs, skill in establishing eligibility, ability to say no to ineligible clients
    D. ability to meet the demands of the case load without too great dependence on supervision, ability to remain objective at all times, skill in case work processes

37. In helping an assistant supervisor select cases for a new worker to carry in his first days with the agency, the MOST important single factor to clarify is that the supervisor must

    A. know the case situation intimately himself
    B. go over the case line-by-line with the worker to be sure the worker has a grasp of the problems presented
    C. select cases that the worker can become readily interested in
    D. select cases that would challenge the worker by the nature of the problem presented

38. Of the following, the MOST appropriate point of view concerning departmental policy and procedure for a supervisor to develop in assistant supervisors is that

    A. they are in the most responsible and strategic spot to influence formulation and revision of policy because they see its effect in practice and have the means of communicating this to the administration
    B. the assistant supervisor must see that the workers carry out policy in every case
    C. they should adapt policy to meet the needs of particular cases not met by any other community resource
    D. they should encourage their workers to provide for the client necessary case action or assistance not covered by departmental policy or procedure

39. Of the following, the MOST important contribution that a supervisor can make to the growth and development of assistant supervisors is to

    A. be available to them whenever they feel a need for consultation
    B. give them definite authority and responsibility for the complete operation of their units, support them in their decisions, and give them help where indicated
    C. have regular conferences with each of them for discussion of problems of unit management or case situations that are too difficult to handle alone
    D. give them a feeling that the supervisor is sharing with them the difficulties of their jobs and is working with them toward a solution of these

40. In reading the case of a worker in her unit, an assistant supervisor finds so many errors in knowledge and judgment and such lack of skill in interviewing that she comes to you for help in dealing with the worker.
    As supervisor, you should advise the assistant supervisor to

    A. let the worker discuss the case as he sees it, discovering the problems on his own
    B. go over the case with the worker, showing up each error and discussing it constructively with him
    C. consider the development and degree of security of the worker, selecting those areas for discussion where the worker will be able to recognize the problems and to handle them constructively himself
    D. discuss the problems bearing on eligibility since these are of primary importance in the Department of Welfare

41. An intake supervisor asks your help in deciding whether a certain client is presumptively eligible to receive assistance. This appears to be an unusual case, and the intake supervisor is experiencing a great deal of difficulty in determining how current policy is applicable to the case. After studying all the data submitted for your inspection, you, the supervisor, find that you also do not know what action should be taken.
    Under the circumstances, you should

    A. instruct the intake supervisor to ask the client for additional information
    B. advise the intake supervisor to accept the case because the benefit of the doubt should be resolved in favor of the applicant
    C. find out what decisions were made in similar cases
    D. ask Case Consultation for an interpretation of the policy to be applied in this case

42. Because of a consistently high rate of applications for assistance and a very active case load situation, it has been necessary to increase the intake department of a large welfare center to twelve intake interviewers, three appointment interviewers, three receptionists, and six service workers. The administrator and you, the supervisor, are planning to request additional supervisory staff.
    Of the following, the MOST feasible action would be to

    A. request an additional assistant supervisor in order to split the responsibilities, having one supervisor over the intake interviewers and the other over the rest of the staff
    B. request the appointment of an assistant supervisor to be responsible for the entire intake department, with two assistant supervisors for direct supervision of the staff
    C. advise Central Office that the Welfare Center is too large and should be split into two
    D. request an additional assistant supervisor and break up the intake section into two departments on a territorial basis, having applicants and clients go to the unit which is responsible for the part of the district in which they live

43. A relatively inexperienced assistant supervisor asks his supervisor to arrange for the reassignment of one of his experienced social investigators because the investigator does not seek or use supervisory help.
    The supervisor should respond to this situation by

A. transferring the social investigator to a unit supervised by a more mature and authoritative person
B. planning a few regular weekly conferences with the assistant supervisor for the purpose of preparing him for his conference with the social investigator
C. refusing to make any reassignment and explaining to the unit supervisor that compliance with his request would not help anyone
D. helping the unit supervisor analyze the investigator's weak points, thereby strengthening the supervisor's position in relation to him

44. One of your assistants, recently assigned as unit supervisor after making a record of effective work as social investigator in getting her clients to meet their problems independently, is having little success in a supervisory role. Her conferences with workers in her unit are superficial, and the workers fail to show signs of any real development.
As supervisor, you should

   A. jointly with her relate the similarities and differences in supervisory and case work relationships to her present and potential methods of supervision
   B. encourage her to use the same techniques that proved successful in her social investigator experience
   C. plan all her future conferences with her so as to broaden their scope and improve her methods
   D. read a block of cases from her unit with her, analyzing the needs of her workers from them in order to demonstrate the superficiality of her approach

45. An assistant supervisor is having difficulty in keeping up with the total demands of his job because nearly all his time is consumed in emergency conferences with social investigators on minor problems they should be able to handle independently.
A wise course of action for the supervisor to follow in this case would be to

   A. help the assistant supervisor realize that he is preventing the proper development of his social investigators by condoning such dependency
   B. advise the assistant supervisor to make himself unavailable to his workers each day until he has accomplished his other tasks
   C. work out with the assistant supervisor a plan of supervision for each of his social investigators
   D. transfer some more experienced workers to the unit in order to relieve the assistant supervisor of some of the pressure imposed on him by the current situation

46. In a certain unit, pending applications are long delayed, reports are not completed on time, statistical studies are unfinished, and the case load is mounting against the trend in the office.
Of the following, the BEST recommendation the supervisor could make to the assistant supervisor in charge of the unit is that the unit supervisor

   A. spend more time on administration and less on supervision
   B. itemize all the things that have to be done and check them off as they are completed
   C. plan a conference with the supervisor by analyzing all the components of the unit-supervising job so that both of them can together work out a suitable time schedule of performance
   D. call a unit meeting and make it clear to all concerned that the backlog of work must be cleared up

47. Mr. Jay, an experienced social investigator, is transferred from another office to a unit under the supervision of Mrs. Emm, a young but capable assistant supervisor on your staff. As supervisor, your advice to Mrs. Emm on the approach to supervising Mr. Jay should be to

    A. give careful, closely controlled supervision until she has had an opportunity to learn his capacities and areas of weakness
    B. let him set the pattern of the relationship in accordance with his feeling of the need for help
    C. arrange for him to conform, as soon as possible, to the normal pattern of supervision found in the unit
    D. evaluate the reference material in relation to the demands of his case load and provide for regular conferences based on this preliminary study

48. As supervisor, you are responsible for the supervision of an assistant supervisor with five years of experience who has been recently transferred to the district.
    You should

    A. tell him to go ahead with his new unit as he had done previously and keep you informed of his progress and difficulties
    B. evaluate his reference material and discuss with him his strengths and weaknesses as you see they will relate to this new assignment
    C. discuss with him his plan for taking hold of the unit and give him such help as seems indicated from his reference material and his approach to the new situation
    D. relate to him as you would to a new supervisor because no two districts are alike and he will need considerable help in making an adjustment

49. An assistant supervisor is seeking help from you in the supervision of a young worker with about one year's experience. The worker is anxious to learn and is making good progress, but recently has shown some resistance and hositility in the supervisory relationship.
    As supervisor, you should

    A. find out what the supervisor is doing to cause this and help her change her methods
    B. find out whether some kind of case problem precipitated this resistant attitude to see if it is a block in learning rather than real irritation at the supervisor
    C. tell the supervisor this is a normal response to supervision at certain times
    D. advise the supervisor to discuss the problem directly with the worker

50. The personnel bureau has asked your office to lend an experienced supervisor for an experimental job in which the individual selected will have to rely on himself, with only occasional direction.
    You, the supervisor, should select the assistant supervisor

    A. whose unit can best take the change to another less competent supervisor for a temporary period
    B. who is interested in being independent, has control of his unit's activity, and is functioning adequately in the supervisor-supervisee relationship
    C. who depends least on you and makes little use of supervision
    D. who is functioning adequately at a certain level but whose potentialities for further growth under supervision are questionable

KEY (CORRECT ANSWERS)

1. D	11. A	21. C	31. A	41. D
2. C	12. A	22. C	32. A	42. B
3. D	13. C	23. C	33. B	43. B
4. D	14. B	24. D	34. A	44. A
5. D	15. B	25. A	35. D	45. A
6. B	16. D	26. C	36. B	46. C
7. D	17. C	27. D	37. A	47. D
8. C	18. A	28. C	38. A	48. C
9. A	19. B	29. A	39. B	49. B
10. C	20. D	30. B	40. C	50. B

EXAMINATION SECTION
TEST 1

DIRECTIONS: Each question or incomplete statement is followed by several suggested answers or completions. Select the one that BEST answers the question or completes the statement. *PRINT THE LETTER OF THE CORRECT ANSWER IN THE SPACE AT THE RIGHT.*

1. It is generally accepted that, of the following, the MOST important medium for developing integration and continuity in learning on the job is
   A. day-to-day experience on the job
   B. the supervisory conference
   C. the staff meeting
   D. the professional seminar

   1._____

2. Assume that you find that one of your workers is over-identifying with a particular client.
   Of the following, the MOST appropriate step for you to take FIRST in dealing with this situation is to
   A. transfer the cases to another worker
   B. inform the worker that he cannot give satisfactory service if he over-identifies with a client
   C. interview the client yourself to determine his feelings about his relationship with the worker
   D. arrange a conference with the worker to discuss the reasons for her over-identification with this client

   2._____

3. The one of the following which is the MOST likely reason why a newly-appointed supervisor would have a tendency to interfere actively in a relationship between one of his workers and a client is that the supervisor
   A. has unresolved feelings about relinquishing the role of worker, and has not yet accepted his role as supervisor
   B. must give direct assistance in the situation because the worker cannot handle it
   C. is attempting to share with his worker the knowledge and skill which he has developed in direct practice
   D. has not realized that immediate responsibility for work with clients has been delegated to others

   3._____

4. A worker who has a tendency to resist authority and supervision can be helped MOST effectively if, of the following, the supervisor
   A. behaves in a strict and impersonal manner so that the worker will accept his authority as a supervisor
   B. modifies the relationship so that he will be less authoritarian and threatening to the worker
   C. gives the worker a simple, matter-of-fact interpretation of the supervisory relationship and has an understanding acceptance of the worker's response
   D. temporarily establishes a peer relationship with the worker in order to overcome his resistance

   4._____

5. Before interviewing a newly-appointed worker for the first time, of the following, it is DESIRABLE for the supervisor to
   A. learn as much as he can about the worker's background and interests in order to eliminate the routine of asking questions and eliciting answers
   B. review the job information to be covered in order to make it easier to be impersonal and keep to the business at hand
   C. send the worker orientation material about the agency and the job and ask him to study it before the interview
   D. review available information about the worker in order to find an area of shared experience to serve as a *taking off* point for getting acquainted

6. In interviewing a new worker, of the following, it is IMPORTANT for the supervisor to
   A. give direction to the progress of the interview and maintain a leadership role throughout
   B. allow the worker to take the initiative in order to give him full scope for freedom of expression
   C. maintain a non-directional approach so that the worker will reveal his true attitudes and feelings
   D. avoid interrupting the worker, even though he seems to want to do all the talking

7. When a new worker, during his first few days, shows such symptoms of insecurity as *stage fright*, helpless immobility, or extreme talkativeness, of the following, it would be MOST helpful for the supervisor to
   A. start the worker out on some activity in which he is relatively secure
   B. ignore the symptoms and allow the worker to *sink or swim* on his own
   C. have a conference with the worker and interpret to him the reasons for his feelings of insecurity
   D. consider the probability that this worker may not be suited for a profession which requires skill in interpersonal relationships

8. Of the following, the MOST desirable method of minimizing workers' dependence on the supervisor and encouraging self-dependence is to
   A. hold group instead of individual supervisory conferences at regular intervals
   B. schedule individual supervisory conferences only in response to the workers' obvious need for guidance
   C. plan for progressive exposure to other opportunities for learning afforded by the agency and the community
   D. allow workers to learn by trial and error rather than by direct supervisory guidance

9. Of the following, it would NOT be appropriate for the supervisor to use early supervisory conferences with the new workers as a means of
   A. giving him direct practical help in order to get going on the job
   B. estimating the level of his native abilities, professional skills and experience
   C. getting clues as to his characteristic ways of learning in a new situation
   D. assessing his potential for future supervisory responsibility

10. Without careful planning by the supervisor for orientation of the new worker, an informal system of orientation by co-workers inevitably develops.
    Such an informal system of orientation is USUALLY
    A. *beneficial*, because many new workers learn more readily when instructed by their peers
    B. *harmful*, because informal orientation by an undesignated co-worker can lead a new worker astray instead of helping him
    C. *beneficial*, because assumption by subordinates of responsibility for orientation will free the supervisor for other urgent work
    D. *harmful*, because such informal orientation by a co-worker will tend to destroy the authority of the supervisor

11. Of the following, the BEST way for a supervisor to assist a subordinate who has unusual work pressures is to
    A. relieve him of some of his cases until the pressures subside
    B. help him to decide which cases should be given the most attention during the period of pressure, and how to provide coverage for less urgent cases
    C. inform him that he must learn to tolerate and adjust to such pressures
    D. point out that he should learn to understand the causes of the pressures, which probably resulted from his own deficiencies

12. Many supervisors have a tendency to use case records mainly for the purpose of analysis of the workers' skill or evaluation of their performance.
    Of the following, a PROBABLE result of this practice is that
    A. workers are likely to tie-in recording with supervisory evaluation of their work, without giving proper emphasis to their importance in improving service to clients
    B. the worker is likely to devote an inordinate amount of time to case records at the expense of his clients
    C. the records are likely to be too lengthy and detailed, limiting their value for other important purposes
    D. the records are likely to be of little value for administrative and research purposes

13. A common obstacle to adequate recording in a large social work agency is the fact that many workers consider recording to be a time-consuming chore. In order to obtain the cooperation of staff in keeping proper records, of the following, it is MOST important for an agency to provide
    A. indisputable evidence of the intelligent use of records as tools in formulating policy and improving service
    B. a system of checks and controls to assure that workers are preparing adequate and timely records
    C. adequate clerical services and mechanical equipment for recording
    D. sufficient time for recording in the organization of every job

14. The one of the following which is NOT a purpose of keeping case records in an agency is
    A. planning
    B. research
    C. training
    D. job classification

15. When a supervisor is reviewing the records of a worker, of the following, he should plan to read
    A. records of new cases only, following up each interview selectively
    B. the total caseload, in order to determine which aspects of the worker's performance should be examined
    C. those records which the worker has brought to the supervisor's attention because of the need for help
    D. a block of records selected according to the worker's need for help, and some records selected at random

16. The one of the following which is the PRIMARY purpose of the regular staff meeting in an agency is
    A. initiation of action in order to get the agency's work done
    B. staff training and development
    C. program and policy determination
    D. communication of new policies and procedures

17. Of the following, group supervision in an agency is intended as a means of
    A. strengthening the total supervisory process
    B. shifting the focus of supervision from the individual to the group
    C. saving costs in terms of time and manpower
    D. influencing policy through group interaction

18. The supervisor's job brings him closer to such limiting factors in the operation of an agency as faulty administrative structure, shortage of funds and lack of facilities, inadequacies in personnel practices, community pressures, and excessive workload.
    For the supervisor to make a practice of communicating to his subordinates his feelings of frustration about such limitations in the work setting would be
    A. *appropriate*, because the worker will be more understanding of the supervisor's burdens and frustrations
    B. *inappropriate*, because the climate created will block rather than further the purposes of supervision
    C. *appropriate*, because such communication will create a more democratic climate between the worker and the supervisor
    D. *inappropriate*, because the supervisor must support and condone agency policies and practices in the presence of subordinates

19. A suggestion has been made that the teaching and administrative functions of supervision should be separated, so that the supervisor responsible for teaching would not be responsible for evaluation of the same workers.
    The one of the following which is the MOST important reason for this point of view is that
    A. elements that confer on the supervisor a position of authority and power unduly threaten the learning situation
    B. teaching skill and administrative ability do not usually go together

C. a supervisor who has been responsible for training a worker is likely to be prejudiced in his favor
D. performance evaluation and total job accountability should be two separate functions

20. In reviewing a worker's cases in preparation for a periodic evaluation, you note that she has done a uniformly good job with certain types of cases and poor work with other types of cases.
Of the following, the BEST approach for you to take in this situation is to
    A. bring this to the worker's attention, find out why she favors certain types of clients, and discuss ways in which she can improve her service to all clients
    B. bring this to the worker's attention and suggest that she may need professional counseling, as she seems to be blocked in working with certain types of cases
    C. assign to her mainly those cases which she handles best and transfer the types of cases which she handles poorly to another worker
    D. accept the fact that a worker cannot be expected to give uniformly good service to all clients, and take no further action

KEY (CORRECT ANSWERS)

1.	B	11.	B
2.	D	12.	A
3.	A	13.	A
4.	C	14.	D
5.	D	15.	D
6.	A	16.	A
7.	A	17.	A
8.	C	18.	B
9.	D	19.	A
10.	B	20.	A

TEST 2

DIRECTIONS: Each question or incomplete statement is followed by several suggested answers or completions. Select the one that BEST answers the question or completes the statement. *PRINT THE LETTER OF THE CORRECT ANSWER IN THE SPACE AT THE RIGHT.*

1. Of the following, the choice of method to be used in the supervisory process should be influenced MOST by the
    A. number and type of cases carried by each worker
    B. emotional maturity of the worker
    C. number of workers supervised and their past experience
    D. subject matter to be learned and the long-range goals of supervision

    1._____

2. In an evaluation conference with a worker, the BEST approach for the supervisor to take is to
    A. help the worker to identify his strengths as a basis for working on his weaknesses
    B. identify the worker's weaknesses and help him overcome them
    C. allow the worker to identify his weaknesses first and then suggest ways of overcoming them
    D. discuss the worker's weaknesses but emphasize his strengths

    2._____

3. Assume that a worker is discouraged about the progress of his work and feels that it is futile to attempt to cope with many of his cases.
   Of the following, it would be BEST for the supervisor to
    A. suggest to the worker that such feelings are inappropriate for a professional worker
    B. tell the worker that he must seek professional help in order to overcome these feelings
    C. reduce the worker's caseload and give him cases that are less complex
    D. review with the worker several of his cases in which there were obvious accomplishments

    3._____

4. The supervisor is responsible for providing the worker with the following means of support, with the EXCEPTION of
    A. interest and advice on his personal problems
    B. instruction on community resources
    C. inspiration for carrying out the work of the agency
    D. understanding his strengths and limitations

    4._____

5. When a worker frequently takes the initiative in asking questions and discussing problems during a supervisory conference, this is PROBABLY an indication that the
    A. supervisor is not sufficiently interested in the work
    B. conference is a positive learning experience for the worker
    C. worker is hostile and resists supervision
    D. supervisor's position of authority is in question

    5._____

6. When a supervisor finds that one of his workers cannot accept criticism, of the following, it would be BEST for the supervisor to
    A. have the worker transferred to another supervisor
    B. warn the worker of disciplinary proceedings unless his attitude changes
    C. have the worker suspended after explaining the reason
    D. explore with the worker his attitude toward authority

6.____

7. Of the following, the condition which the inexperienced worker is LEAST likely to be aware of, without the guidance of the supervisor, is
    A. when he is successful in helping a client
    B. when he is not making progress in helping a client
    C. that he has a personal bias toward certain clients
    D. that he feels insecure because of lack of experience

7.____

8. The supervisor should provide an inexperienced worker with controls as well as freedom MAINLY because controls will
    A. enable him to set up his own controls sooner
    B. put him in a situation which is closer to the realities of life
    C. help him to use authority in handling a casework problem
    D. give him a feeling of security and lay the foundation for future self-direction

8.____

9. A result of the use of summarized case recording by the worker is that it
    A. gives the supervisor more responsibility for selecting cases to discuss in conference
    B. makes more time available for other activities
    C. lowers the morale of many workers
    D. decreases discussion of cases by the worker and the supervisor

9.____

10. The distinction between the role of professional workers and the role of auxiliary or sub-professional workers in an agency is based upon the
    A. position within the agency hierarchy
    B. amount of close supervision given
    C. emergent nature of tasks assigned
    D. functions performed

10.____

11. Of the following, the MOST important source of learning for the worker should be
    A. departmental directives and professional literature
    B. his co-workers in the agency
    C. the content of in-service training courses
    D. the clients in his caseload

11.____

12. A client is MOST likely to feel that he is receiving acceptance and understanding if the social worker
    A. gets detailed information about the client's problem
    B. demonstrates that he realistically understands the client's problem
    C. has an intellectual understanding of the client's problem
    D. offers the client assurance of assistance

12.____

13. A client will be MORE encouraged to speak freely about his problems if the worker
    A. avoids asking too many questions
    B. asks leading rather than pointed questions
    C. suggests possible answers
    D. identifies with the client

14. A client would be MOST likely to be able to accept help in a time of crisis and need if the worker
    A. explains agency policy to him
    B. responds immediately to the client's need
    C. explains why help cannot be given immediately
    D. reaches out to help the client establish his rightful claim for assistance

15. It is a generally accepted principle that the worker should interpret for himself what the client is saying, but usually should not pass his interpretation on to the client because the client
    A. will become hostile to the worker
    B. should arrive at his own conclusions at his own pace
    C. must request the interpretation first
    D. usually wants facts, rather than the worker's interpretation

16. In evaluating the client's capacity to cope with his problems, it is MOST important for the worker to assess his ability to
    A. form close relationships   B. ask for help
    C. express his hostility   D. verbalize his difficulties

17. When a worker finds that he disagrees strongly with an agency policy, it is DESIRABLE for him to
    A. share his feelings about the policy with his client
    B. understand fully why he has such strong feelings about the policy
    C. refer cases involving the policy to his supervisor
    D. refuse to give help in cases involving the policy

18. Which of the following practices is BEST for a supervisor to use when assigning work to his staff?
    A. Give workers with seniority the most difficult jobs
    B. Assign all unimportant work to the slower workers
    C. Permit each employee to pick the job he prefers
    D. Make assignments based on the workers' abilities

19. In which of the following instances is a supervisor MOST justified in giving commands to people under his supervision?
    When
    A. they delay in following instructions which have been given to them clearly
    B. they become relaxed and slow about work, and he wants to speed up their production
    C. he must direct them in an emergency situation
    D. he is instructing them on jobs that are unfamiliar to them

20. Which of the following supervisory actions or attitudes is MOST likely to result in getting subordinates to try to do as much work as possible for a supervisor?
He
    A. shows that his most important interest is in schedules and production goals
    B. consistently pressures his staff to get the work out
    C. never fails to let them know he is in charge
    D. considers their abilities and needs while requiring that production goals be met

20.____

KEY (CORRECT ANSWERS)

1.	D	11.	D
2.	A	12.	B
3.	D	13.	D
4.	A	14.	D
5.	B	15.	B
6.	D	16.	A
7.	C	17.	B
8.	D	18.	D
9.	B	19.	C
10.	D	20.	D

TEST 3

DIRECTIONS: Each question or incomplete statement is followed by several suggested answers or completions. Select the one that BEST answers the question or completes the statement. *PRINT THE LETTER OF THE CORRECT ANSWER IN THE SPACE AT THE RIGHT.*

1. One of your workers comes to you and complains in an angry manner about your having chosen him for some particular assignment. In your opinion, the subject of the complaint is trivial land unimportant, but it seems to be quite important to your worker.
   The BEST of the following actions for you to take in this situation is to
   A. allow the worker to continue talking until he has calmed down and then explain the reasons for your having chosen him for that particular assignment
   B. warn the worker to moderate his tone of voice at once because he is bordering on insubordination
   C. tell the worker in a friendly tone that he is making a tremendous fuss over an extremely minor matter
   D. point out to the worker that you are his immediate supervisor and that you are running the unit in accordance with official policy

   1.____

2. The one of the following which is the LEAST desirable action for an assistant supervisor to take in disciplining a subordinate for an infraction of the rules is to
   A. caution him against repetition of the infraction, even if it is minor
   B. point out his progress in applying the rules at the same time that you reprimand him
   C. be as specific as possible in reprimanding him for rule infractions
   D. allow a cooling-off period to elapse before reprimanding him

   2.____

3. A training program for workers assigned to the intake section should include actual practice in simulated interviews under simulated conditions.
   The one of the following educational principles which is the CHIEF justification for this statement is that
   A. the workers will remember what they see better and longer than what they read or hear
   B. the workers will learn more effectively by actually doing the act themselves than they would learn from watching others do it
   C. the conduct of simulated interviews once or twice will enable them to cope with the real situation with little difficulty
   D. a training program must employ methods of a practical nature if the workers are to find anything of lasting value in it

   3.____

4. In order for a supervisor to employ the system of democratic leadership in his supervision, it would generally be BEST for him to
   A. allow his subordinates to assist in deciding on methods of work performance and job assignments but only in those areas where decisions have not been made on higher administrative levels

   4.____

B. allow his subordinates to decide how to do the required work, interposing his authority when work is not completed on schedule or is improperly completed
C. attempt to make assignments of work to individuals only of the type which they enjoy doing
D. maintain control over job assignment and work production, but allow the subordinates to select methods of work and internal conditions of work at democratically conducted staff conferences

5. In a unit in which supervision has been considered quite effective, it has become necessary to press for above-normal production for a limited period to achieve a required goal.
The one of the following which is a LEAST likely result of this pressure is that
    A. there will be more *griping* by employees
    B. some workers will do both more and better work than has been normal for them
    C. there will be an enhanced feeling of group unity
    D. there will be increased absenteeism

5._____

6. For a supervisor to encourage competitive feelings among his staff is
    A. *advisable*, chiefly because the workers will perform more efficiently when they have proper motivation
    B. *inadvisable*, chiefly because the workers will not perform well under the pressure of competition
    C. *advisable*, chiefly because the workers will have a greater incentive to perform their job properly
    D. *inadvisable*, chiefly because the workers may focus their attention on areas where they excel and neglect other essential aspects of the job

6._____

7. In selecting jobs to be assigned to a new worker, the supervisor should assign those jobs which
    A. give the worker the greatest variety of experience
    B. offer the worker the greatest opportunity to achieve concrete results
    C. present the worker with the greatest stimulation because of their interesting nature
    D. require the least amount of contact with outside agencies

7._____

8. A supervisor should avoid a detailed discussion of a worker-client interview with a new worker before the worker has fully recorded the interview CHIEFLY because such a discussion might
    A. cover matters which are already fully covered and explained in the written record
    B. make the worker forget some important deal learned during the interview
    C. color the recording according to the worker's reaction to his supervisor's opinions
    D. minimize the worker's feeling of having reached a decision independently

8._____

9. Some supervisors encourage their worker to submit a list of their questions about specific jobs or their comments about problems they wish to discuss in advance of the worker-supervisor conference.
This practice is
   A. *desirable*, chiefly because it helps to stimulate and focus the worker's thinking about his caseload
   B. *undesirable*, chiefly because it will stifle the worker's free expression of his problems and attitudes
   C. *desirable*, chiefly because it will allow the conference to move along more smoothly and quickly
   D. *undesirable*, chiefly because it will restrict the scope of the conference and the variety of jobs discussed

9.____

10. An alert supervisor hears a worker apparently giving the wrong information to a client and immediately reprimands him severely.
For the supervisor to reprimand the worker at his point is poor CHIEFLY because
   A. instruction must precede correct performance
   B. oral reprimands are less effective than written reprimands
   C. the worker was given no opportunity to explain his reasons for what he did
   D. more effective training can be obtained by discussing the errors with a group of workers

10.____

11. The one of the following circumstances when it would generally be MOST proper for a supervisor to do a job himself rather than to train a subordinate to do the job is when it is
   A. a job which the supervisor enjoys doing and does well
   B. not a very time-consuming job but an important one
   C. difficult to train another to do the job, yet is not difficult for the supervisor to do
   D. unlikely that this or any similar job will have to be done again at any future time

11.____

12. Effective training of subordinates requires that the supervisor understand certain facts about learning and forgetting processes.
Among these is the fact that people GENERALLY
   A. forget what they learned at a much greater rate during the first day than during subsequent periods
   B. both learn and forget at a relatively constant rate and this rate is dependent upon their general intellectual capacity
   C. learn at a relatively constant rate except for periods of assimilation when the quantity of retained learning decreases while information is becoming firmly fixed in the mind
   D. learn very slowly at first when introduced to a new topic, after which there is a great increase in the rate of learning

12.____

13. It has been suggested that a subordinate who likes his superior will tend to do better work than one who does not.
According to the MOST widely held current theories of supervision, this suggestion is a
    A. *bad* one, since personal relationships tend to interfere with proper professional relationships
    B. *bad* one, since the strongest motivating factors are fear and uncertainty
    C. *good* one, since liking one's superior is a motivating factor for good work performance
    D. *good* one, since liking one's supervisor is the most important factor in employee performance

14. One factor which might be given consideration in deciding upon the optimum span of control of a supervisor over his immediate subordinates is the position of the supervisor in the hierarchy of the organization.
It is generally considered proper that the number of subordinates immediately supervised by a higher, upper echelon supervisor _____ the number supervised by lower level supervisors.
    A. is unrelated to and tends to form no pattern with
    B. should be about the same as
    C. should be larger than
    D. should be smaller than

15. The one of the following instances when it is MOST important for an upper level supervisor to follow the chain of command is when he is
    A. communicating decisions   B. communicating information
    C. receiving suggestions   D. seeking information

16. At the end of his probationary period, a supervisor should be considered potentially valuable in his position if he shows
    A. awareness of his areas of strength and weakness, identification with the administration of the department, and ability to learn under supervision
    B. skill in work, supervision, and administration, and a friendly democratic approach to the staff
    C. knowledge of departmental policies and procedures and ability to carry them out, ability to use authority, and ability to direct the work of the staff
    D. an identification with the department, acceptance of responsibility, and ability to give help to the individuals who are to be supervised

17. Good supervision is selective because
    A. it is not necessary to direct all the activities of the person
    B. a supervisor would never have time to know the whole caseload of a worker
    C. workers resent too much help from a supervisor
    D. too much reading is a waste of valuable time

18. An important administrative problem is how precisely to define the limits of authority that is delegated to subordinate supervisors.
Such definition of limits of authority should be
   A. as precise as possible and practicable in all areas
   B. as precise as possible and practicable in areas of function, but should allow considerable flexibility in the area of personnel management
   C. as precise as possible and practicable in the area
   D. of personnel management, but should allow considerable flexibility in the areas of function
   E. in general terms so as to allow considerable flexibility both in the areas of function and in the areas of personnel management

19. Experts in the field of personnel relations feel that it is generally a bad practice for subordinate employees to become aware of pending or contemplated changes in policy or organizational set-up via the *grapevine* CHIEFLY because
   A. evidence that one or more responsible officials have proved untrustworthy will undermine confidence in the agency
   B. the information disseminated by this method is seldom entirely accurate and generally spreads needless unrest among the subordinate staff
   C. the subordinate staff may conclude that the administration feels the staff cannot be trusted with the true information
   D. the subordinate staff may conclude that the administration lacks the courage to make an unpopular announcement through official channels

20. Supervision is subject to many interpretations, depending on the area in which it functions.
Of the following, the statement which represents the MOST appropriate meaning of supervision as it is known in social work practice is that it
   A. is a leadership process for the development of new leaders
   B. is an educational and administrative process aimed at teaching personnel the goal of improved service to the client
   C. is an activity aimed chiefly at insuring that workers will adhere to all agency directives
   D. provides the opportunity for administration to secure staff reaction to agency policies

21. A supervisor may utilize various methods in the supervisory process.
The one of the following upon which sound supervisory practice rests in the selection of supervisory techniques is
   A. an estimate of the worker arrived at through current and past evaluation of performance as well as through worker's participation
   B. the previous supervisor's evaluation and recommendation
   C. the worker's expression of his personal preference for certain types of experience
   D. the amount of time available to supervisor and supervisee

22. It is the practice of some supervisors, when they believe that it would be desirable for a subordinate to take a particular action in a case, to inform the subordinate of this in the form of a suggestion rather than in the form of a direct order.
In general, this method of getting a subordinate to take the desired action is
   A. *inadvisable*; it may create in the mind of the subordinate the impression that the supervisor is uncertain about the efficacy of her plan and is trying to avoid whatever responsibility she may have in resolving the case
   B. *advisable*; it provides the subordinate with the maximum opportunity to use her own judgment in handling the case
   C. *inadvisable*; it provides the subordinate with no clear-cut direction and, therefore, is likely to leave her with a feeling of uncertainty and frustration
   D. *advisable*; it presents the supervisor's view in a manner which will be most likely to evoke the subordinate's cooperation

22.____

23. A veteran supervisor noticed that one of her workers of average ability had begun developing some bad work habits, becoming especially careless in her recordkeeping. After reprimand from the supervisor, the investigator corrected her errors and has been doing satisfactory work since then.
For the supervisor to keep referring to this period of poor work during her weekly conferences with this employee would generally be considered poor personnel practice CHIEFLY because
   A. praise rather than criticism is generally the best method to use in improving the work of an unsatisfactory worker
   B. the supervisor cannot know whether the employee's errors will follow an established pattern
   C. the fault which evoked the original negative criticism no longer exists
   D. this would tend to frustrate the worker by making her strive overly hard to reach a level of productivity which is beyond her ability to achieve

23.____

24. Assume that you are now a supervisor in a specific unit. Two experienced investigators in your unit, both of whom do above average work, have for some time not gotten along with each other for personal reasons Their attitude toward one another has suddenly become hostile and noisy disagreement has taken place in the office.
The BEST action for you to take FIRST in this situation is to
   A. transfer one of the two investigators to another unit where contact with the other investigator will be unnecessary
   B. discuss the problem with the two investigators together, insisting that they confide in you and tell you the cause of their mutual antagonism
   C. confer with the two investigators separately, pointing out to each the need to adopt an adult professional attitude with respect to their on-the-job relations
   D. advise the two investigators that should the situation grow worse, disciplinary action will be considered

24.____

25. It has long been recognized that relationships exist between worker morale and working conditions.
The one of the following which BEST clarifies these existing relationships is that morale is
   A. affected for better or worse in direct relationship to the magnitude of the changes in working conditions for better or worse
   B. better when working conditions are better
   C. little affected by working conditions so long as the working conditions do not approach the intolerable
   D. more affected by the degree of interest shown in providing good working conditions than by the actual conditions and may, perversely, be highest when working conditions are worst

KEY (CORRECT ANSWERS)

1.	A	11.	D
2.	D	12.	A
3.	B	13.	C
4.	A	14.	D
5.	D	15.	A
6.	D	16.	D
7.	B	17.	A
8.	C	18.	A
9.	A	19.	B
10.	C	20.	B

21. A
22. D
23. C
24. C
25. D

INTERVIEWING
EXAMINATION SECTION
TEST 1

DIRECTIONS: Each question or incomplete statement is followed by several suggested answers or completions. Select the one that BEST answers the question or completes the statement. *PRINT THE LETTER OF THE CORRECT ANSWER IN THE SPACE AT THE RIGHT.*

1. Of the following, the BEST way for an interviewer to calm a person who seems to have become emotionally upset as a result of a question asked is for the interviewer to

    A. talk to the person about other things for a short time
    B. ask that the person control himself
    C. probe for the cause of his emotional upset
    D. finish the questioning as quickly as possible

    1._____

2. You find that an applicant is hesitant about showing you some required personal material and documents. Your *initial* reaction to this situation should be to

    A. quietly insist that he give you the required materials
    B. make an exception in his case to avoid making him uncomfortable
    C. suspect that he may be trying to withhold evidence
    D. understand that he is in a stressful situation and may feel ashamed to reveal such information

    2._____

3. An applicant has just given you a response which does not seem clear.
Of the following, the BEST course of action for you to take in order to check your understanding of the applicant's response is for you to

    A. ask the question again during a subsequent interview with this applicant
    B. repeat the applicant's answer in the applicant's own words and ask if that is what the applicant meant
    C. later in the interview, repeat the question that led to this response
    D. repeat the question that led to this response, but say it more forcefully

    3._____

4. While speaking with applicants, you may find that there are times when an applicant will be silent for a short while before answering questions.
In order to gather the best information from the applicant, the interviewer should *generally* treat these silences by

    A. repeating the same question to make the applicant stop hesitating
    B. rephrasing the question in a way that the applicant can answer it faster
    C. directing an easier question to the applicant so that he can gain confidence in answering
    D. waiting patiently and not pressuring the applicant into quick, undeveloped answers

    4._____

5. In dealing with members of *different* ethnic and religious groups among the applicants you interview, you should give

    A. individuals the services to which they are entitled
    B. less service to those you judge to be more advantaged

    5._____

C. better service to groups with which you sympathize most
D. better service to groups with political "muscle"

6. You must be sure that, when interviewing an applicant, you phrase each question carefully.
Of the following, the MOST important reason for this is to insure that

   A. the applicant will phrase each of his responses carefully
   B. you use correct grammar
   C. it is clear to the applicant what information you are seeking
   D. you do not word the same question differently for different applicants

7. When given a form to complete, a client hesitates, tells you that he cannot fill out forms too well and that he is afraid he will do a poor job. He asks you to do it for him. You are quite sure, however, that he is able to do it himself.
In this case, it would be MOST advisable for you to

   A. encourage him to try filling out the application as well as he can
   B. fill out the application for him
   C. explain to him that he must learn to accept responsibility
   D. tell him that, if others can fill out an application, he can too

8. Assume that an applicant whom you are interviewing has made a statement that is obviously not true.
Of the following, the BEST course of action for you to take at this point in the interview is to

   A. ask the applicant if he is sure about his statement
   B. tell the applicant that his statement is incorrect
   C. question the applicant further to clarify his response
   D. assume that the statement is correct

9. Assume that you are conducting an *initial* interview with an applicant.
Of the following, the MOST advisable questions for you to ask at the beginning of this interview are those that

   A. can be answered in one or two sentences
   B. have nothing to do with the subject matter of the interview
   C. are most likely to reveal any hostility on the part of the applicant
   D. the applicant is most likely to be willing and able to answer

10. When interviewing a particularly nervous and upset applicant, the one of the following actions which you should take FIRST is to

    A. inform the applicant that, to be helped, he must cooperate
    B. advise the applicant that proof must be provided for statements he makes
    C. assure the applicant that every effort will be made to provide him with whatever assistance he is entitled to
    D. tell the applicant he will have no trouble so long as he is truthful

11. Assume that it is part of your job to prepare a monthly report for your unit head that eventually goes to the director. The report contains information on the number of applicants you have interviewed that have been approved and the number of applicants you have interviewed that have been turned down. Errors on such reports are *serious* because

    A. you are expected to be able to prove how many applicants you have interviewed each month
    B. accurate statistics are needed for effective management of the department
    C. they may not be discovered before the report is transmitted to the director
    D. they may result in a loss to the applicants left out of the report

11.____

12. During interviews, people give information about themselves in several ways. Which of the following *usually* gives the LEAST amount of information about the person being questioned? His

    A. spoken words
    B. tone of voice
    C. facial expression
    D. body position

12.____

13. Suppose an applicant, while being interviewed, becomes angered by your questioning and begins to use sharp, uncontrolled language.
    Which of the following is the BEST way for you to react to him?

    A. Speak in his style to show him that you are neither impressed nor upset by his speech
    B. Interrupt him and tell him that you are not required to listen to this kind of speech
    C. Lower your voice and slow the rate of your speech in an attempt to set an example that will calm him
    D. Let him continue in his way but insist that he answer your questions directly

13.____

14. You have been informed that no determination has yet been made on the eligibility of an applicant whom you have interviewed. The decision depends on further checking. His situation, however, is similar to that of many other applicants whose eligibility has been approved. The applicant, *quite worried,* calls you, and asks whether his application has been accepted.
    What would be BEST for you to do under these circumstances? Tell him

    A. his application is being checked and you will let him know the final result as soon as possible
    B. that a written request addressed to your supervisor will probably get faster action for his case
    C. not to worry since other applicants with similar backgrounds have already been accepted
    D. since there is no definite information and you are very busy, you will call him back

14.____

15. Suppose that you have been talking with an applicant. You have the feeling from the latest things the applicant has said that some of his answers to earlier questions were not totally correct. You guess that he might have been afraid or confused earlier but that your conversation has now put him in a more comfortable frame of mind.
    In order to test the reliability of information received from the earlier questions, the BEST thing for you to do *now* is to ask new questions that

15.____

A. allow the applicant to explain why he deliberately gave false information to you
B. ask for the same information, although worded differently from the original questions
C. put pressure on the applicant so that he personally wants to clear up the facts in his earlier answers
D. indicate to the applicant that you are aware of his deceptiveness

16. While providing you with required information, an applicant whom you are interviewing, informs you that she does not know certain facts.
Of the following, the MOST advisable action for you to take is to

    A. ask her to explain further
    B. advise her about research facilities
    C. express your sympathy for the situation
    D. go on to the next item of information

17. If, in an interview, you wish to determine a client's usual occupation, which one of the following questions is MOST likely to elicit the *most* useful information?

    A. Did you ever work in a factory?
    B. Do you know how to do office work?
    C. What kind of work do you do?
    D. Where are you working now?

18. Assume that you are approached by a clerk from another office who starts questioning you about one of the clients you have just interviewed. The clerk says that she is a relative of the client. According to departmental policy, all matters discussed with clients are to be kept confidential.
Of the following, the BEST course of action for you to take in this situation would be to

    A. check to see whether the clerk is really a relative before you make any further decisions
    B. explain to the clerk why you cannot divulge the information
    C. tell the clerk that you do not know the answers to her questions
    D. tell the clerk that she can get from the client any information the client wishes to give

19. Which of the following is usually the BEST technique for you, as an interviewer, to use to bring an applicant back to subject matter from which the applicant has strayed?

    A. Ask the applicant a question that is related to the subject of the interview
    B. Show the applicant that his response is unrelated to the question
    C. Discreetly reind the applicant that there is a time allotment for the interview
    D. Tell the applicant that you will be happy to discuss the extraneous matters at a future interview

20. Assume that you are interviewing a witness who is telling a story crucial to your investigation. It is important that you get all the facts being related by this witness. In order to secure this vital information, the BEST of the following techniques is to

    A. quietly interrupt the witness's story and request him to speak with deliberation so that you can record his statement
    B. guide the witness during his recital so that all important points are validated

C. confine your activities during the story to brief note-taking, and, after the information has been secured, request a full written statement
D. inform the witness that he must relate all the facts as truthfully and concisely as possible

21. The statement of any witness obtained in an interview should GENERALLY be considered

    A. as a lead requiring substantiation by additional evidence
    B. accurate if the witness appears honest and is cooperative
    C. unreliable if the witness has been involved in similar investigations
    D. as a fact admissible under the rules of evidence

22. During an important interview, an interviewer takes notes from time to time but very rarely looks at the subject being questioned.
    Such action on the part of the interviewer is

    A. *unacceptable,* chiefly because during the actual interview an interviewer should pay more attention to the witness's manner of giving the information rather than to the content of his statements
    B. *acceptable,* chiefly because data should be recorded at the earliest opportunity and important data should be noted meticulously
    C. *unacceptable,* chiefly because it inhibits the person being interviewed and is not conducive to a give-and-take discussion
    D. *unacceptable,* chiefly because focusing attention on note-taking and not on the person being interviewed creates an impression of professional objectivity

23. Since he must interview persons with various personalities and attitudes, an interviewer should, *generally,* adopt a method of interviewing that

    A. is uniformly applicable to all types so that discrepancies in the accounts of individuals may be readily detected
    B. can be adjusted to the persons whom he interviews
    C. is based on the premise that most interviewees tend to be uncooperative
    D. requires the interviewer to spend as little time as possible in questioning applicants

24. One of the more difficult tasks facing an interviewer is to control the tendency of witnesses to ramble when giving information.
    Of the following, the BEST technique for keeping a witness's comments pertinent is to

    A. ask questions which indicate the desired answer
    B. insist on "yes" and "no" answers to his questions
    C. construct questions that restrict the range of information which the witness can give in response
    D. ask precise questions so that the answers of the witness will necessarily be brief

25. During interviews, a certain interviewer phrases follow-up questions mentally during pauses while the subject is still answering the previous question. This practice is, *generally,*

    A. *desirable,* chiefly because it gives the impression that the interviewer is well acquainted with all the facts
    B. *undesirable,* chiefly because the interviewer cannot know whether such questions will be appropriate
    C. *desirable,* chiefly because it enables the interviewer to pose new questions without significant breaks in the discussion
    D. *undesirable,* chiefly because it subjects the person being interviewed to a barrage of questions

KEY (CORRECT ANSWERS)

1. A
2. D
3. B
4. D
5. A

6. C
7. A
8. C
9. D
10. C

11. B
12. D
13. C
14. A
15. B

16. D
17. C
18. B
19. A
20. C

21. A
22. C
23. B
24. C
25. C

TEST 2

DIRECTIONS: Each question or incomplete statement is followed by several suggested answers or completions. Select the one that BEST answers the question or completes the statement. *PRINT THE LETTER OF THE CORRECT ANSWER IN THE SPACE AT THE RIGHT.*

1. The one of the following which is the BEST description of a *properly* objective interviewer is one who

    A. is friendly and sensitive to the client's feelings, without becoming emotionally involved
    B. is distant and impersonal, remaining unaffected by what the client says
    C. lets personal emotions enter as far as the client's situation calls for them
    D. becomes emotionally involved with the client's situation, but without showing this involvement

    1.____

2. The one of the following which is MOST necessary for successfully intefviewing a person who belongs to a culture different from that of the interviewer is for the interviewer to

    A. have some appreciation of the other culture
    B. ignore those cultural differences which lead to bias
    C. stay away from sensitive, "touchy" issues
    D. assume the mannerisms of people in the other culture

    2.____

3. In fact-finding interviews, it is generally assumed that the smaller the lumber of interviewees, the greater the increase of reliability with the addition of others.
   The PROPER number of interviewees needed to insure the accuracy of information obtained *generally* depends upon the

    A. educational level of those interviewed
    B. number of people who have the required information
    C. directness of the questions asked
    D. variability of the information received

    3.____

4. The one of the following which is generally MOST likely to be *accurately* described in an interview by an interviewee is

    A. the presence of a large painting in the interviewer's office
    B. the number of people in the interviewer's waiting room
    C. space relations
    D. duration of time

    4.____

5. The one of the following which is *generally* the BEST course of action for an interviewer to take when interviewing a person who is reluctant to tell what he knows about a matter under investigation is to

    A. be curt and abrupt, and threaten the person with the consequences of his withholding information
    B. be firm and severe, and pressure the person into telling the needed information

    5.____

C. be patient and candid with the person being questioned about the investigation since doing otherwise is not ethical
D. give the person false information about the investigation so he will give the needed information without realizing its importance

6. It is often recommended that an interviewer prepare in advance a list of questions or topics to be covered in an interview.
The MAIN reason for using such a checklist is to

   A. allow investigations to be assigned to less efficient interviewers
   B. eliminate a large amount of follow-up paper work
   C. aid the interviewer in remembering to cover all important topics
   D. aid the interviewer in maintaining an objective distance from the person interviewed

7. *Usually,* the CHIEF advantage of a directive approach in an interview is that the

   A. interviewer maintains control over the course of the interview
   B. person interviewed is more likely to be put at ease
   C. person interviewed is generally left free to direct the interview
   D. interviewer will not suggest answers to the person interviewed

8. *Usually,* the CHIEF advantage of a non-directive approach in conducting an interview is that the

   A. interviewer generally conceals what he is looking for in the interview
   B. person interviewed is more likely to express his true feelings about the topic under discussion
   C. person interviewed is more likely to follow an idea introduced by the interviewer
   D. interviewer can keep the discussion limited to topics he believes to be relevant

9. The one of the following which is generally the LEAST likely to be *accurate* in a description of an event given to an interviewer is a statement about

   A. the presence of an object
   B. the number of people, when their number is small
   C. locations of people
   D. duration of time

10. Assume that you, an interviewer, are conducting a character investigation.
In an interview, the one of the following character traits of the person being interviewed which can *usually* be determined with a GOOD degree of reliability is

    A. honesty   B. dependability
    C. forcefulness   D. perseverance

11. You have been assigned the task of obtaining a family's social history.
The BEST place for you to interview members of the family while obtaining this social history would, *generally,* be in

    A. the family's home
    B. your agency's general offices
    C. the home of a friend of the family
    D. your own private office

12. If an interviewer obtains testimony from persons in interviews by means of interrogation or asking questions rather than by letting the person freely relate the testimony, what is said will, *generally*, be

    A. *greater* in range and *less* accurate
    B. *greater* in range and *more* accurate
    C. about the *same* in range and *less* accurate
    D. about the *same* in range and *more* accurate

13. Experienced interviewers have learned to phrase their questions carefully in order to obtain the desired response. Of the following, the question which would *usually* elicit the MOST accurate answer is:

    A. "How old are you?"
    B. "What is your income?"
    C. "How are you today?"
    D. "What is your date of birth?"

14. The one of the following questions which would *generally* lead to the LEAST reliable answer is:

    A. "Did you see a wallet?"
    B. "Was the German Shepherd gray?"
    C. "Didn't you see the stop sign?"
    D. "Did you see the guard on duty?"

15. Some interviewers may make a practice of observing details of the surroundings when interviewing in someone's home or office.
    Such a practice is, *generally*, considered

    A. *undesirable,* mainly because such snooping is an unwarranted, unethical invasion of privacy
    B. *undesirable,* mainly because useful information is rarely, if ever, gained this way
    C. *desirable,* mainly because useful insights into the character of the person interviewed may be gained
    D. *desirable,* mainly because it is impossible to evaluate a person adequately without such observation of his environment

KEY (CORRECT ANSWERS)

1. A	6. C	11. A
2. A	7. A	12. A
3. D	8. B	13. D
4. A	9. D	14. B
5. C	10. C	15. C

PREPARING WRITTEN MATERIAL

PARAGRAPH REARRANGEMENT
COMMENTARY

The sentences that follow are in scrambled order. You are to rearrange them in proper order and indicate the letter choice containing the correct answer at the space at the right.

Each group of sentences in this section is actually a paragraph presented in scrambled order. Each sentence in the group has a place in that paragraph; no sentence is to be left out. You are to read each group of sentences and decide upon the best order in which to put the sentences so as to form a well-organized paragraph.

The questions in this section measure the ability to solve a problem when all the facts relevant to its solution are not given.

More specifically, certain positions of responsibility and authority require the employee to discover connection between events sometimes, apparently, unrelated. In order to do this, the employee will find it necessary to correctly infer that unspecified events have probably occurred or are likely to occur. This ability becomes especially important when action must be taken on incomplete information.

Accordingly, these questions require competitors to choose among several suggested alternatives, each of which presents a different sequential arrangement of the events. Competitors must choose the MOST logical of the suggested sequences.

In order to do so, they may be required to draw on general knowledge to infer missing concepts or events that are essential to sequencing the given events. Competitors should be careful to infer only what is essential to the sequence. The plausibility of the wrong alternatives will always require the inclusion of unlikely events or of additional chains of events which are NOT essential to sequencing the given events.

It's very important to remember that you are looking for the best of the four possible choices, and that the best choice of all may not even be one of the answers you're given to choose from.

There is no one right way to solve these problems. Many people have found it helpful to first write out the order of the sentences, as they would have arranged them, on their scrap paper before looking at the possible answers. If their optimum answer is there, this can save them some time. If it isn't, this method can still give insight into solving the problem. Others find it most helpful to just go through each of the possible choices, contrasting each as they go along. You should use whatever method feels comfortable and works for you.

While most of these types of questions are not that difficult, we've added a higher percentage of the difficult type, just to give you more practice. Usually there are only one or two questions on this section that contain such subtle distinctions that you're unable to answer confidently. And you then may find yourself stuck deciding between two possible choices, neither of which you're sure about.

EXAMINATION SECTION
TEST 1

DIRECTIONS: The sentences that follow are in scrambled order. You are to rearrange them in proper order and indicate the letter choice containing the correct answer. *PRINT THE LETTER OF THE CORRECT ANSWER IN THE SPACE AT THE RIGHT.*

1. Below are four statements labeled W, X, Y and Z. 1.____
   W. He was a strict and fanatic drillmaster.
   X. The word is always used in a derogatory sense and generally shows resentment and anger on the part of the user.
   Y. It is from the name of this Frenchman that we derive our English word, martinet.
   Z. Jean Martinet was the Inspector-General of Infantry during the reign of King Louis XIV.
   The PROPER order in which these sentences should be placed in a paragraph is:
   A. X, Z, W, Y   B. X, Z, Y, W   C. Z, W, Y, X   D. Z, Y, W, X

2. In the following paragraph, the sentences, which are numbered, have been jumbled. 2.____
   I. Since then it has undergone changes.
   II. It was incorporated in 1955 under the laws of the State of New York.
   III. Its primary purposes, a cleaner city, has, however, remained the same.
   IV. The Citizens Committee works in cooperation with the Mayor's Interdepartmental Committee for a Clean City. 3.____
   The order in which these sentences should be arranged to form a well-organized paragraph is:
   A. II, IV, I, III   B. III, IV, I, II   C. IV, II, I, III   D. IV, III, II, I

Questions 3-5.

DIRECTIONS: The sentences listed below are part of a meaningful paragraph but they are not given in their proper order. You are to decide what would be the BEST order in which to put the sentences so as to form a well-organized paragraph. Each sentence has a place in the paragraph; there are no extra sentences. You are then to answer Questions 3 through 5 inclusive on the basis of your rearrangements of these scrambled sentences into a properly organized paragraph.

In 1887 some insurance companies organized an Inspection Department to advise their clients on all phases of fire prevention and protection. Probably this has been due to the smaller annual fire losses in Great Britain than in the United States. It tests various fire prevention devices and appliances and determines manufacturing hazards and their safeguards. Fire research began earlier in the United States and is more advanced than in Great Britain. Later they established a laboratory specializing in electrical, mechanical, hydraulic, and chemical fields.

111

2 (#1)

3. When the five sentences are arranged in proper order, the paragraph starts with the sentence which begins
   A. "In 1887…"   B. "Probably this…"   C. "It tests…"
   D. "Fire research…"   E. "Later they…"

3.____

4. In the last sentence listed above, "they" refers to
   A. the insurance companies
   B. the United States and Great Britain
   C. the Inspection Department
   D. clients
   E. technicians

4.____

5. When the above paragraph is properly arranged, it ends with the words
   A. "…and protection."
   B. "…the United States."
   C. "…their safeguards."
   D. "…in Great Britain."
   E. "…chemical fields."

5.____

KEY (CORRECT ANSWERS)

1. C
2. C
3. D
4. A
5. C

TEST 2

DIRECTIONS: In each of the questions numbered I through V, several sentences are given. For each question, choose as your answer the group of number that represents the MOST logical order of these sentences if they were arranged in paragraph form. *PRINT THE LETTER OF THE CORRECT ANSWER IN THE SPACE AT THE RIGHT.*

1.
   I. It is established when one shows that the landlord has prevented the tenant's enjoyment of his interest in the property leased.
   II. Constructive eviction is the result of a breach of the covenant of quiet enjoyment implied in all leases.
   III. In some parts of the United States, it is not complete until the tenant vacates within a reasonable time.
   IV. Generally, the acts must be of such serious and permanent character as to deny the tenant the enjoyment of his possessing rights.
   V. In this event, upon abandonment of the premises, the tenant's liability for that ceases.
   The CORRECT answer is:
   A. II, I, IV, III, V
   B. V, II, III, I, IV
   C. IV, III, I, II, V
   D. I, III, V, IV, II

   1.____

2.
   I. The powerlessness before private and public authorities that is the typical experience of the slum tenant is reminiscent of the situation of blue-collar workers all through the nineteenth century.
   II. Similarly, in recent years, this chapter of history has been reopened by anti-poverty groups which have attempted to organize slum tenants to enable them to bargain collectively with their landlords about the conditions of their tenancies.
   III. It is familiar history that many of the worker remedied their condition by joining together and presenting their demands collectively.
   IV. Like the workers, tenants are forced by the conditions of modern life into substantial dependence on these who possess great political aid and economic power.
   V. What's more, the very fact of dependence coupled with an absence of education and self-confidence makes them hesitant and unable to stand up for what they need from those in power.
   The CORRECT answer is:
   A. V, IV, I, II, III
   B. II, III, I, V, IV
   C. III, I, V, IV, II
   D. I, IV, V, III, II

   2.____

3.
   I. A railroad, for example, when not acting as a common carrier may contract away responsibility for its own negligence.
   II. As to a landlord, however, no decision has been found relating to the legal effect of a clause shifting the statutory duty of repair to the tenant.
   III. The courts have not passed on the validity of clauses relieving the landlord of this duty and liability.
   IV. They have, however, upheld the validity of exculpatory clauses in other types of contracts.

   3.____

V. Housing regulations impose a duty upon the landlord to maintain leased premises in safe condition.
VI. As another example, a bailee may limit his liability except for gross negligence, willful acts, or fraud.

The CORRECT answer is:
A. II, I, VI, IV, III, V
B. I, III, IV, V, VI, II
C. III, V, I, IV, II, VI
D. V, III, IV, I, VI, II

4.
I. Since there are only samples in the building, retail or consumer sales are generally eschewed by mart occupants, and in some instances, rigid controls are maintained to limit entrance to the mart only to those persons engaged in retailing.
II. Since World War I, in many larger cities, there has developed a new type of property, called the mart building.
III. It can, therefore, be used by wholesalers and jobbers for the display of sample merchandise.
IV. This type of building is most frequently a multi-storied, finished interior property which is a cross between a retail arcade and a loft building.
V. This limitation enables the mart occupants to ship the orders from another location after the retailer or dealer makes his selection from the samples.

The CORRECT answer is:
A. II, IV, III, I, V
B. IV, III, V, I, II
C. I, III, II, IV, V
D. I, IV, II, III, V

5.
I. In general, staff-line friction reduces the distinctive contribution of staff personnel.
II. The conflicts, however, introduce an uncontrolled element into the managerial system.
III. On the other hand, the natural resistance of the line to staff innovations probably usefully restrains over-eager efforts to apply untested procedures on a large scale.
IV. Under such conditions, it is difficult to know when valuable ideas are being sacrificed.
V. The relatively weak position of staff, requiring accommodation to the line, tends to restrict their ability to engage in free, experimental innovation.

The CORRECT answer is:
A. IV, II, III, I, V
B. I, V, III, II, IV
C. V, III, I, II, IV
D. II, I, IV, V, III

KEY (CORRECT ANSWERS)

1. A
2. D
3. D
4. A
5. B

TEST 3

DIRECTIONS: Questions 1 through 4 consist of six sentences which can be arranged in a logical sequence. For each question, select the choice which places the numbered sentences in the MOST logical sequent. *PRINT THE LETTER OF THE CORRECT ANSWER IN THE SPACE AT THE RIGHT.*

1. I. The burden of proof as to each issue is determined before trial and remains upon the same party throughout the trial.
    II. The jury is at liberty to believe one witness' testimony as against a number of contradictory witnesses.
    III. In a civil case, the party bearing the burden of proof is required to prove his contention by a fair preponderance of the evidence.
    IV. However, it must be noted that a fair preponderance of evidence does not necessarily mean a greater number of witnesses.
    V. The burden of proof is the burden which rests upon one of the parties to an action to persuade the trier of the facts, generally the jury, that a proposition he asserts is true.
    VI. If the evidence is equally balanced, or if it leaves the jury in such doubt as to be unable to decide the controversy either way, judgment must be given against the party upon whom the burden of proof rests.
    The CORRECT answer is:
    A. III, II, V, IV, I, VI   B. I, II, VI, V, III, IV
    C. III, IV, V, I, II, VI   D. V, I, III, VI, IV, II

    1.____

2. I. If a parent is without assets and is unemployed, he cannot be convicted of the crime of non-support of a child.
    II. The term "sufficient ability" has been held to mean sufficient financial ability.
    III. It does not matter if his unemployment is by choice or unavoidable circumstances.
    IV. If he fails to take any steps at all, he may be liable to prosecution for endangering the welfare of a child.
    V. Under the penal law, a parent is responsible for the support of his minor child only if the parent is "of sufficient ability."
    VI. An indigent parent may meet his obligation by borrowing money or by seeking aid under the provisions of the Social Welfare Law.
    The CORRECT answer is:
    A. VI, I, V, III, II, IV   B. I, III, V, II, IV, VI
    C. V, II, I, III, VI, IV   D. I, VI, IV, V, II, III

    2.____

3. I. Consider, for example, the case of a rabble rouser who urges a group of twenty people to go out and break the windows of a nearby factory.
    II. Therefore, the law fills the indicated gap with the crime of inciting to riot.
    III. A person is considered guilty of inciting to riot when he urges ten or more persons to engage in tumultuous and violent conduct of a kind likely to create public alarm.
    IV. However, if he has not obtained the cooperation of at least four people, he cannot be charged with unlawful assembly.

    3.____

2 (#3)

V. The charge of inciting to riot was added to the law to cover types of conduct which cannot be classified as either the crime of "riot" or the crime of "unlawful assembly."
VI. If he acquires the acquiescence of at least four of them, he is guilty of unlawful assembly even if the project does not materialize.

The CORRECT answer is:
A. III, V, I, VI, IV, II
B. V, I, IV, VI, II, III
C. III, IV, I, V, II, VI
D. V, I, IV, VI, III, II

4. I. If, however, the rebuttal evidence presents an issue of credibility, it is for the jury to determine whether the presumption has, in fact, been destroyed.
   II. Once sufficient evidence to the contrary is introduced, the presumption disappears from the trial.
   III. The effect of a presumption is to place the burden upon the adversary to come forward with evidence to rebut the presumption.
   IV. When a presumption is overcome and ceases to exist in the case, the fact or facts which gave rise to the presumption still remain.
   V. Whether a presumption has been overcome is ordinarily a question for the court.
   VI. Such information may furnish a basis for a logical inference.

The CORRECT answer is:
A. IV, VI, II, V, I, III
B. III, II, V, I, IV, VI
C. V, III, VI, IV, II, I
D. V, IV, I, II, VI, III

4._____

KEY (CORRECT ANSWERS)

1. D
2. C
3. A
4. B

PREPARING WRITTEN MATERIAL
EXAMINATION SECTION
TEST 1

DIRECTIONS: Each of the following sentences may be classified under one of the following four categories:
A. *Faulty* because of incorrect grammar or usage
B. *Faulty* because of incorrect punctuation or spelling
C. *Faulty* because of incorrect capitalization
D. *Correct*

Examine each sentence carefully. Then, in the correspondingly numbered space on the right, print the capital letter preceding the option which is the best of the four suggested above.

(All incorrect sentences contain but one type of error. Consider a sentence correct if it contains none of the types of errors mentioned, even though there may be other correct ways of expressing the same thought.

1. They gave the poor man some food when he approached.   1.____
2. I regret the loss caused by the error.   2.____
3. The students have a new teacher for shop mantenance.   3.____
4. They sweared to bring out all the facts.   4.____
5. He decided to open a branch store on 33rd street.   5.____
6. His speed is equal and more than that of a racehorse.   6.____
7. He felt very warm on that Summer day.   7.____
8. He was assisted by his friend, who lives in the next house.   8.____
9. The climate of New York is colder than California.   9.____
10. I shall wait for you on the corner.   10.____
11. Did we see the boy whose the leader?   11.____
12. Being a modest person, John seldom takes about his invention.   12.____
13. The gang is called the smith street boys.   13.____
14. He seen the man break into the store.   14.____

2 (#1)

15. We expected to lay still there for quite a while.   15._____
16. He is considered to be the Leader of his organization.   16._____
17. Although He received an invitation, He won't go.   17._____
18. The letter must be here some place.   18._____
19. I thought it to be he.   19._____
20. We expect to remain here for a long time.   20._____
21. The committee was agreed.   21._____
22. Two-thirds of the building are finished.   22._____
23. The water was froze.   23._____
24. Everyone of the salesmen must supply their own car.   24._____
25. Who is the author of Gone With the Wind?   25._____
26. He marched on and declaring that he would never surrender.   26._____
27. Who shall I say called?   27._____
28. Everyone has left but they.   28._____
29. Who did we give the order to?   29._____
30. Send your order in immediately.   30._____
31. I believe I paid the Bill.   31._____
32. I have not met but one person.   32._____
33. Why aren't Tom, and Fred, going to the dance?   33._____
34. What reason is there for him not going?   34._____
35. The seige of Malta was a tremendous event.   35._____
36. I was there yesterday I assure you.   36._____
37. Your ukulele is better than mine.   37._____
38. No one was there only Mary.   38._____

3 (#1)

39. The Capital city of Vermont is Montpelier. 39.____

40. Reggie Jackson may hit the largest amount of home runs this season. 40.____

KEY (CORRECT ANSWERS)

1. B	11. B	21. D	31. C
2. D	12. D	22. A	32. A
3. B	13. C	23. A	33. B
4. A	14. A	24. A	34. A
5. C	15. A	25. B	35. B
6. A	16. C	26. A	36. B
7. C	17. C	27. D	37. B
8. D	18. A	28. D	38. A
9. A	19. A	29. A	39. C
10. D	20. D	30. D	40. A

TEST 2

Questions 1-3.

DIRECTIONS: Questions 1 through 3 each consist of four sentences. Choose the one sentence in each set of four that would be BEST for a formal letter or report. Consider grammar and appropriate usage.

1. A. Most all the work he completed before he become ill.
   B. He completed most of the work before becoming ill.
   C. Prior to him becoming ill his work was mostly completed.
   D. Before he became will most of the work he had completed.

   1.____

2. A. Being that the report lacked a clearly worded recommendation, it did not matter that it contained enough information.
   B. There was enough information in the report, although it, including the recommendation, were not clearly worded.
   C. Although the report contained enough information, it did not have a clearly worded recommendation.
   D. Though the report did not have a recommendation that was clearly worded, and the information therein contained was enough.

   2.____

3. A. Having already overlooked the important mistakes, the ones which she found were not as important toward the end of the letter.
   B. Toward the end of the letter she had already overlooked the important mistakes, so that which she had found were not important.
   C. The mistakes which she had already overlooked were not as important as those which near the end of letter she had found.
   D. The mistakes which she found near the end of the letter were not so important as those which she had already overlooked.

   3.____

Questions 4-5.

DIRECTIONS: Select the correct answer.

4. The unit has exceeded _____ goals and the employees are satisfied with _____ accomplishments.
   A. their; it's   B. it's, it's   C. is, there   D. its, their

   4.____

5. Research indicates that employees who _____ no opportunity for close social relationships often find their work unsatisfying, and this _____ of satisfaction often reflects itself in low production.
   A. have, lack   B. have, excess   C. has, lack   D. has, excess

   5.____

KEY (CORRECT ANSWERS)

1. B
2. C
3. D
4. D
5. A

TEST 3

DIRECTIONS: Select the choice which BEST expresses the thought and which contains NO errors in grammar or sentence construction.

1.
   A. She, hearing a signal, the source lamp flashed.
   B. While hearing a signal, the source lamp flashed
   C. In hearing a signal, the source lamp flashed.
   D. As she heard a signal, the source lamp flashed.

   1.____

2.
   A. Every one of the time records have been initialed in the designated spaces.
   B. All of the time records has been initialed in the designated spaces.
   C. Which one of the time records was initialed in the designated spaces.
   D. The time records all been initialed in the designated spaces.

   2.____

3.
   A. If there is no one else to answer the phone, you will have to answer it.
   B. You will have to answer it yourself if no one else answers the phone.
   C. If no one else is not around to pick up the phone, you have to do it.
   D. You will have to answer the phone when nobodys here to do it.

   3.____

4.
   A. Dr. Byrnes not in his office. What could I do for you?
   B. Dr. Byrnes is not in his office. Is there something I can do for you?
   C. Since Dr. Byrnes is not in his office, might there be something I may do for you?
   D. Is there any ways I can assist you since Dr. Brynes is not in his office?

   4.____

5.
   A. She do not understand how the new console works.
   B. The way the new console works, she doesn't understand.
   C. She doesn't understand how the new console works.
   D. The new console works, so that she doesn't understand.

   5.____

KEY (CORRECT ANSWERS)

1. D
2. C
3. A
4. B
5. C

TEST 4

DIRECTIONS: The following questions each consist of a sentence which may or may not be an example of good English usage.

Consider grammar, punctuation, spelling, capitalization, awkwardness, etc.

Examine each sentence and then choose the correct statement about it from the four choices below. If the English usage in the sentence given is better than any of the changes suggested in options B, C, or D, choose option A. (Do not choose an option that will change the meaning of the sentence.)

1. The typist used an extention cord in order to connect her typewriter to the outlet nearest to her desk.
   A. This is an example of acceptable writing.
   B. A period should be placed after the word "cord" and the word "in" should have a capital "I."
   C. A comma should be placed after the word "typewriter."
   D. The word "extention" should be spelled "extension."

2. He would have went to the conference if he had received an invitation.
   A. This is an example of acceptable writing.
   B. The word "went" should be replaced by the word "gone."
   C. The word "had" should be replaced by "would have."
   D. The word "conference" should be spelled "conference."

3. In order to make the report neater, he spent many hours rewriting it.
   A. This is an example of acceptable writing.
   B. The word "more" should be inserted before the word "neater."
   C. There should be a colon after the word "neater."
   D. The word "spent" should be changed to "have spent."

4. His supervisor told him that he should of read the memorandum more carefully.
   A. This is an example of acceptable writing.
   B. The word "memorandum" should be spelled "memorandom."
   C. The word "of" should be replaced by the word "have."
   D. The word "carefully" should be replaced by the word "have."

5. It was decided that two separate reports should be written.
   A. This is an example of acceptable writing.
   B. A comma should be inserted after the word "decided."
   C. The word "be" should be replaced by the word "been."
   D. A colon should be inserted after the word "that."

6. She don't seem to understand that the work must be done as soon as possible.
   A. This is an example of acceptable writing.
   B. The word "doesn't" should replace the word "don't."
   C. The word "why" should replace the word "that."
   D. The word "as" before the word "soon" should be eliminated.

KEY (CORRECT ANSWERS)

1. D
2. B
3. A
4. C
5. A
6. B

PREPARING WRITTEN MATERIAL

EXAMINATION SECTION

TEST 1

DIRECTIONS: Each question or incomplete statement is followed by several suggested answers or completions. Select the one that BEST answers the question or completes the statement. *PRINT THE LETTER OF THE CORRECT ANSWER IN THE SPACE AT THE RIGHT.*

Questions 1-4.

DIRECTIONS: Questions 1 through 4 each consist of a sentence which may or may not be an example of good English. The underlined parts of each sentence may be correct or incorrect. Examine each sentence, considering grammar, punctuation, spelling, and capitalization. If the English usage in the underlined parts of the sentence given is better than any of the changes in the underlined words suggested in options B, C, or D, choose option A. If the changes in the underlined words suggested in options B, C, or D would make the sentence correct, choose the correct option. Do not choose an option that will change the meaning of the sentence.

1. This Fall, the office will be closed on Columbus Day, October 9th.   1.____
   A. Correct as is
   B. fall...Columbus Day; October
   C. Fall...columbus day, October
   D. fall...Columbus Day – October

2. There weren't no paper in the supply closet.   2.____
   A. Correct as is
   B. weren't any
   C. wasn't any
   D. wasn't no

3. The alphabet, or A to Z sequence are the basis of most filing systems.   3.____
   A. Correct as is
   B. alphabet, or A to Z sequence, is
   C. alphabet, or A to Z sequence, are
   D. alphabet, or A too Z sequence, is

4. The Office Aide checked the register and finding the date of the meeting.   4.____
   A. Correct as is
   B. regaster and finding
   C. register and found
   D. regaster and found

Questions 5-10.

DIRECTIONS: Questions 5 through 10 consist of sentences which contain examples of correct or incorrect English usage. Examine each sentence with reference to grammar, spelling, punctuation, and capitalization. Chooses one of the following options that would be BEST for correct English usage:

125

A. The sentence is correct
B. There is one mistake
C. There are two mistakes
D. There are three mistakes

5. Mrs. Fitzgerald came to the 59th Precinct to retreive her property which were stolen earlier in the week.   5.____

6. The two officer's responded to the call, only to find that the perpatrator and the victim have left the scene.   6.____

7. Mr. Coleman called the 61st Precinct to report that, upon arriving at his store, he discovered that there was a large hole in the wall and that three boxes of radios were missing.   7.____

8. The Administrative Leiutenant of the 62nd Precinct held a meeting which was attended by all the civilians, assigned to the Precinct.   8.____

9. Three days after the robbery occurred the detective apprahended two suspects and recovered the stolen items.   9.____

10. The Community Affairs Officer of the 64th Precinct is the liaison between the Precinct and the community; he works closely with various community organizations, and elected officials,   10.____

Questions 11-18.

DIRECTIONS: Questions 11 through 18 are to be answered on the basis of the following paragraph, which contains some deliberate errors in spelling and/or grammar and/or punctuation. Each line of the paragraph is preceded by a number. There are 9 lines and 9 numbers.

Line No.	Paragraph Line
1	The protection of life and proporty are, one of
2	the oldest and most important functions of a city.
3	New York City has it's own full-time police Agency.
4	The police Department has the power an it shall
5	be there duty to preserve the Public piece,
6	prevent crime detect and arrest offenders, supress
7	riots, protect the rites of persons and property, etc.
8	The maintainance of sound relations with the community they
9	serve is an important function of law enforcement officers

11. How many errors are contained in line one?   11.____

12. How many errors are contained in line two?   12.____

13. How many errors are contained in line three?   13.____

14. How many errors are contained in line four? 14._____

15. How many errors are contained in line five? 15._____

16. How many errors are contained in line six? 16._____

17. How many errors are contained in line seven? 17._____

18. How many errors are contained in line eight? 18._____

19. In the sentence, *The candidate wants to file his application for preference before it is too late*, the word *before* is used as a(n) 19._____
    A. preposition
    B. subordinating conjunction
    C. pronoun
    D. adverb

20. The one of the following sentences which is grammatically PREFERABLE to the others is: 20._____
    A. Our engineers will go over your blueprints so that you may have no problems in construction.
    B. For a long time he had been arguing that we, not he, are to blame for the confusion.
    C. I worked on this automobile for two hours and still cannot find out what is wrong with it.
    D. Accustomed to all kinds of hardships, fatigue seldom bothers veteran policemen.

KEY (CORRECT ANSWERS)

1.	A	11.	C
2.	C	12.	D
3.	B	13.	C
4.	C	14.	B
5.	C	15.	C
6.	D	16.	B
7.	A	17.	A
8.	C	18.	A
9.	C	19.	B
10.	B	20.	A

TEST 2

DIRECTIONS: Each question or incomplete statement is followed by several suggested answers or completions. Select the one that BEST answers the question or completes the statement. *PRINT THE LETTER OF THE CORRECT ANSWER IN THE SPACE AT THE RIGHT.*

1. The plural of
   A. turkey is turkies
   B. cargo is cargoes
   C. bankruptcy is bankruptcys
   D. son-in-law is son-in-laws

   1.____

2. The abbreviation *viz.* means MOST NEARLY
   A. namely   B. for example   C. the following   D. see

   2.____

3. In the sentence, *A man in a light-grey suit waited thirty-five minutes in the ante-room for the all-important document,* the word IMPROPERLY hyphenated is
   A. light-grey   B. thirty-five   C. ante-room   D. all-important

   3.____

4. The MOST accurate of the following sentences is:
   A. The commissioner, as well as his deputy and various bureau heads, were present.
   B. A new organization of employers and employees have been formed.
   C. One or the other of these men have been selected.
   D. The number of pages in the book is enough to discourage a reader.

   4.____

5. The MOST accurate of the following sentences is:
   A. Between you and me, I think he is the better man.
   B. He was believed to be me.
   C. Is it us that you wish to see?
   D. The winners are him and her.

   5.____

Questions 6-13.

DIRECTIONS: The sentences numbered 6 through 13 deal with some phase of police activity. They may be classified most appropriately under one of the following four categories.

   A. Faulty because of incorrect grammar
   B. Faulty because of incorrect punctuation
   C. Faulty because of incorrect use of a word
   D. Correct

Examine each sentence carefully. Then, in the space at the right, print the capital letter preceding the option which is the BEST of the four suggested above. All incorrect sentences contain only one type of error. Consider a sentence correct if it contains none of the types of errors mentioned, even though there may be other correct ways of expressing the same thought.

2 (#2)

6. The Department Medal of Honor is awarded to a member of the Police Force who distinguishes himself inconspicuously in the line of police duty by the performance of an act of gallantry.

6._____

7. Members of the Detective Division are charged with the prevention of crime, the detection and arrest of criminals and the recovery of lost or stolen property,

7._____

8. Detectives are selected from the uniformed patrol forces after they have indicated by conduct, aptitude and performance that they are qualified for the more intricate duties of a detective.

8._____

9. The patrolman, pursuing his assailant, exchanged shots with the gunman and immortally wounded him as he fled into a nearby building.

9._____

10. The members of the Traffic Division has to enforce the Vehicle and Traffic Law, the Traffic Regulations and ordinances relating to vehicular and pedestrian traffic.

10._____

11. After firing a shot at the gunman, the crowd dispersed from the patrolman's line of fire.

11._____

12. The efficiency of the Missing Persons Bureau is maintained with a maximum of public personnel due to the specialized training given to its members.

12._____

13. Records of persons arrested for violations of Vehicle and Traffic Regulations are transmitted upon request to precincts, courts and other authorized agencies.

13._____

14. Following are two sentences which may or may not be written in correct English:
    I. Two clients assaulted the officer.
    II. The van is illegally parked.
   Which one of the following statements is CORRECT?
    A. Only Sentence I is written in correct English.
    B. Only Sentence II is written in correct English.
    C. Sentences I and II are both written in correct English.
    D. Neither Sentence I nor Sentence II is written in correct English.

14._____

15. Following are two sentences which may or may not be written in correct English:
    I. Security Officer Rollo escorted the visitor to the patrolroom.
    II. Two entry were made in the facility logbook.
   Which one of the following statements is CORRECT?
    A. Only Sentence I is written in correct English.
    B. Only Sentence II is written in correct English.
    C. Sentences I and II are both written in correct English.
    D. Neither Sentence I nor Sentence II is written in correct English.

15._____

16. Following are two sentences which may or may not be written in correct English:
    I. Officer McElroy putted out a small fire in the wastepaper basket.
    II. Special Officer Janssen told the visitor where he could obtained a pass.
    Which one of the following statements is CORRECT?
    A. Only Sentence I is written in correct English.
    B. Only Sentence II is written in correct English.
    C. Sentences I and II are both written in correct English.
    D. Neither Sentence I nor Sentence II is written in correct English.

17. Following are two sentences which may or may not be written in correct English:
    I. Security Officer Warren observed a broken window while he was on his post in Hallway C.
    II. The worker reported that two typewriters had been stolen from the office,
    Which one of the following statements is CORRECT?
    A. Only Sentence I is written in correct English.
    B. Only Sentence II is written in correct English.
    C. Sentences I and II are both written in correct English.
    D. Neither Sentence I nor Sentence II is written in correct English,

18. Following are two sentences which may or may not be written in correct English:
    I. Special Officer Cleveland was attempting to calm an emotionally disturbed visitor.
    II. The visitor did not stop crying and calling for his wife.
    Which one of the following statements is CORRECT?
    A. Only Sentence I is written in correct English.
    B. Only Sentence II is written in correct English.
    C. Sentences I and II are both written in correct English.
    D. Neither Sentence I nor Sentence II is written in correct English.

19. Following are two sentences that may or may not be written in correct English:
    I. While on patrol, I observes a vagrant loitering near the drug dispensary.
    II. I escorted the vagrant out of the building and off the premises.
    Which one of the following statements is CORRECT?
    A. Only Sentence I is written in correct English.
    B. Only Sentence II is written in correct English.
    C. Sentences I and II are both written in correct English.
    D. Neither Sentence I nor Sentence II is written in correct English.

20. Following are two sentences which may or may not be written in correct English:
    I. At 4:00 P.M., Sergeant Raymond told me to evacuate the waiting area immediately due to a bomb threat.
    II. Some of the clients did not want to leave the building.
    Which one of the following statements is CORRECT?
    A. Only Sentence I is written in correct English.
    B. Only Sentence II is written in correct English.
    C. Sentences I and II are both written in correct English.
    D. Neither Sentence I nor Sentence II is written in correct English.

KEY (CORRECT ANSWERS)

1.	B	11.	A
2.	A	12.	C
3.	C	13.	D
4.	D	14.	C
5.	A	15.	A
6.	C	16.	D
7.	B	17.	A
8.	D	18.	A
9.	C	19.	B
10.	A	20.	C

PHILOSOPHY, PRINCIPLES, PRACTICES, AND TECHNICS
OF
SUPERVISION, ADMINISTRATION, MANAGEMENT, AND ORGANIZATION

TABLE OF CONTENTS

	Page
MEANING OF SUPERVISION	1
THE OLD AND THE NEW SUPERVISION	1
THE EIGHT (8) BASIC PRINCIPLES OF THE NEW SUPERVISION	1
I. Principle of Responsibility	1
II. Principle of Authority	2
III. Principle of Self-Growth	2
IV. Principle of Individual Worth	2
V. Principle of Creative Leadership	2
VI. Principle of Success and Failure	2
VII. Principle of Science	3
VIII. Principle of Cooperation	3
WHAT IS ADMINISTRATION?	3
I. Practices Commonly Classed as "Supervisory"	3
II. Practices Commonly Classed as "Administrative"	3
III. Practices Commonly Classed as Both "Supervisory" and "Administrative"	4
RESPONSIBILITIES OF THE SUPERVISOR	4
COMPETENCIES OF THE SUPERVISOR	4
THE PROFESSIONAL SUPERVISOR-EMPLOYEE RELATIONSHIP	4
MINI-TEXT IN SUPERVISION, ADMINISTRATION, MANAGEMENT, AND ORGANIZATION	5
I. Brief Highlights	5
A. Levels of Management	6
B. What the Supervisor Must Learn	6
C. A Definition of Supervision	6
D. Elements of the Team Concept	6
E. Principles of Organization	6
F. The Four Important Parts of Every Job	7
G. Principles of Delegation	7
H. Principles of Effective Communications	7
I. Principles of Work Improvement	7
J. Areas of Job Improvement	7
K. Seven Key Points in Making Improvements	8

	L.	Corrective Techniques for Job Improvement	8
	M.	A Planning Checklist	8
	N.	Five Characteristics of Good Directions	9
	O.	Types of Directions	9
	P.	Controls	9
	Q.	Orienting the New Employee	9
	R.	Checklist for Orienting New Employees	9
	S.	Principles of Learning	10
	T.	Causes of Poor Performance	10
	U.	Four Major Steps in On-the-Job Instructions	10
	V.	Employees Want Five Things	10
	W.	Some Don'ts in Regard to Praise	11
	X.	How to Gain Your Workers' Confidence	11
	Y.	Sources of Employee Problems	11
	Z.	The Supervisor's Key to Discipline	11
	AA.	Five Important Processes of Management	12
	BB.	When the Supervisor Fails to Plan	12
	CC.	Fourteen General Principles of Management	12
	DD.	Change	12
II.	Brief Topical Summaries		13
	A.	Who/What is the Supervisor?	13
	B.	The Sociology of Work	13
	C.	Principles and Practices of Supervision	14
	D.	Dynamic Leadership	14
	E.	Processes for Solving Problems	15
	F.	Training for Results	15
	G.	Health, Safety, and Accident Prevention	16
	H.	Equal Employment Opportunity	16
	I.	Improving Communications	16
	J.	Self-Development	17
	K.	Teaching and Training	17
		1. The Teaching Process	17
		a. Preparation	17
		b. Presentation	18
		c. Summary	18
		d. Application	18
		e. Evaluation	18
		2. Teaching Methods	18
		a. Lecture	18
		b. Discussion	18
		c. Demonstration	19
		d. Performance	19
		e. Which Method to Use	19

PHILOSOPHY, PRINCIPLES, PRACTICES, AND TECHNICS
OF
SUPERVISION, ADMINISTRATION, MANAGEMENT, AND ORGANIZATION

MEANING OF SUPERVISION

The extension of the democratic philosophy has been accompanied by an extension in the scope of supervision. Modern leaders and supervisors no longer think of supervision in the narrow sense of being confined chiefly to visiting employees, supplying materials, or rating the staff. They regard supervision as being intimately related to all the concerned agencies of society, they speak of the supervisor's function in terms of "growth," rather than the "improvement" of employees.

This modern concept of supervision may be defined as follows: Supervision is leadership and the development of leadership within groups which are cooperatively engaged in inspection, research, training, guidance, and evaluation.

THE OLD AND THE NEW SUPERVISION

TRADITIONAL
1. Inspection
2. Focused on the employee
3. Visitation
4. Random and haphazard
5. Imposed and authoritarian
6. One person usually

MODERN
1. Study and analysis
2. Focused on aims, materials, methods, supervisors, employees, environment
3. Demonstrations, intervisitation, workshops, directed reading, bulletins, etc.
4. Definitely organized and planned (scientific)
5. Cooperative and democratic
6. Many persons involved (creative)

THE EIGHT (8) BASIC PRINCIPLES OF THE NEW SUPERVISION

I. Principle of Responsibility
   Authority to act and responsibility for acting must be joined.
   A. If you give responsibility, give authority.
   B. Define employee duties clearly.
   C. Protect employees from criticism by others.
   D. Recognize the rights as well as obligations of employees.
   E. Achieve the aims of a democratic society insofar as it is possible within the area of your work.
   F. Establish a situation favorable to training and learning.
   G. Accept ultimate responsibility for everything done in your section, unit, office, division, department.
   H. Good administration and good supervision are inseparable.

II. Principle of Authority
The success of the supervisor is measured by the extent to which the power of authority is not used.
  A. Exercise simplicity and informality in supervision
  B. Use the simplest machinery of supervision
  C. If it is good for the organization as a whole, it is probably justified.
  D. Seldom be arbitrary or authoritative.
  E. Do not base your work on the power of position or of personality.
  F. Permit and encourage the free expression of opinions.

III. Principle of Self-Growth
The success of the supervisor is measured by the extent to which, and the speed with which, he is no longer needed.
  A. Base criticism on principles, not on specifics.
  B. Point out higher activities to employees.
  C. Train for self-thinking by employees to meet new situations.
  D. Stimulate initiative, self-reliance, and individual responsibility
  E. Concentrate on stimulating the growth of employees rather than on removing defects.

IV. Principle of Individual Worth
Respect for the individual is a paramount consideration in supervision.
  A. Be human and sympathetic in dealing with employees.
  B. Don't nag about things to be done.
  C. Recognize the individual differences among employees and seek opportunities to permit best expression of each personality.

V. Principle of Creative Leadership
The best supervision is that which is not apparent to the employee.
  A. Stimulate, don't drive employees to creative action.
  B. Emphasize doing good things.
  C. Encourage employees to do what they do best.
  D. Do not be too greatly concerned with details of subject or method.
  E. Do not be concerned exclusively with immediate problems and activities.
  F. Reveal higher activities and make them both desired and maximally possible.
  G. Determine procedures in the light of each situation but see that these are derived from a sound basic philosophy.
  H. Aid, inspire, and lead so as to liberate the creative spirit latent in all good employees.

VI. Principle of Success and Failure
There are no unsuccessful employees, only unsuccessful supervisors who have failed to give proper leadership.
  A. Adapt suggestions to the capacities, attitudes, and prejudices of employees.
  B. Be gradual, be progressive, be persistent.
  C. Help the employee find the general principle; have the employee apply his own problem to the general principle.
  D. Give adequate appreciation for good work and honest effort.
  E. Anticipate employee difficulties and help to prevent them.
  F. Encourage employees to do the desirable things they will do anyway.
  G. Judge your supervision by the results it secures.

VII. Principle of Science
Successful supervision is scientific, objective, and experimental. It is based on facts, not on prejudices.
- A. Be cumulative in results.
- B. Never divorce your suggestions from the goals of training.
- C. Don't be impatient of results.
- D. Keep all matters on a professional, not a personal, level.
- E. Do not be concerned exclusively with immediate problems and activities.
- F. Use objective means of determining achievement and rating where possible.

VIII. Principle of Cooperation
Supervision is a cooperative enterprise between supervisor and employee.
- A. Begin with conditions as they are.
- B. Ask opinions of all involved when formulating policies.
- C. Organization is as good as its weakest link.
- D. Let employees help to determine policies and department programs.
- E. Be approachable and accessible—physically and mentally.
- F. Develop pleasant social relationships.

WHAT IS ADMINISTRATION

Administration is concerned with providing the environment, the material facilities, and the operational procedures that will promote the maximum growth and development of supervisors and employees. (Organization is an aspect and a concomitant of administration.)

There is no sharp line of demarcation between supervision and administration; these functions are intimately interrelated and, often, overlapping. They are complementary activities.

I. Practices Commonly Classed as "Supervisory"
- A. Conducting employees' conferences
- B. Visiting sections, units, offices, divisions, departments
- C. Arranging for demonstrations
- D. Examining plans
- E. Suggesting professional reading
- F. Interpreting bulletins
- G. Recommending in-service training courses
- H. Encouraging experimentation
- I. Appraising employee morale
- J. Providing for intervisitation

II. Practices Commonly Classified as "Administrative"
- A. Management of the office
- B. Arrangement of schedules for extra duties
- C. Assignment of rooms or areas
- D. Distribution of supplies
- E. Keeping records and reports
- F. Care of audio-visual materials
- G. Keeping inventory records
- H. Checking record cards and books

I. Programming special activities
J. Checking on the attendance and punctuality of employees

III. Practices Commonly Classified as Both "Supervisory" and "Administrative"
A. Program construction
B. Testing or evaluating outcomes
C. Personnel accounting
D. Ordering instructional materials

RESPONSIBILITIES OF THE SUPERVISOR

A person employed in a supervisory capacity must constantly be able to improve his own efficiency and ability. He represent the employer to the employees and only continuous self-examination can make him a capable supervisor.

Leadership and training are the supervisor's responsibility. An efficient working unit is one in which the employees work with the supervisor. It is his job to bring out the best in his employees. He must always be relaxed, courteous, and calm in his association with his employees. Their feelings are important, and a harsh attitude does not develop the most efficient employees.

COMPETENCES OF THE SUPERVISOR

I. Complete knowledge of the duties and responsibilities of his position.
II. To be able to organize a job, plan ahead, and carry through.
III. To have self-confidence and initiative.
IV. To be able to handle the unexpected situation and make quick decisions.
V. To be able to properly train subordinates in the positions they are best suited for.
VI. To be able to keep good human relations among his subordinates.
VII. To be able to keep good human relations between his subordinates and himself and to earn their respect and trust.

THE PROFESSIONAL SUPERVISOR-EMPLOYEE RELATIONSHIP

There are two kinds of efficiency: one kind is only apparent and is produced in organizations through the exercise of mere discipline; this is but a simulation of the second, or true, efficiency which springs from spontaneous cooperation. If you are a manager, no matter how great or small your responsibility, it is your job, in the final analysis, to create and develop this involuntary cooperation among the people whom you supervise. For, no matter how powerful a combination of money, machines, and materials a company may have, this is a dead and sterile thing without a team of willing, thinking, and articulate people to guide it.

The following 21 points are presented as indicative of the exemplary basic relationship that should exist between supervisor and employee:

1. Each person wants to be liked and respected by his fellow employee and wants to be treated with consideration and respect by his superior.
2. The most competent employee will make an error. However, in a unit where good relations exist between the supervisor and his employees, tenseness and fear do not exist. Thus, errors are not hidden or covered up, and the efficiency of a unit is not impaired.

3. Subordinates resent rules, regulations, or orders that are unreasonable or unexplained.
4. Subordinates are quick to resent unfairness, harshness, injustices, and favoritism.
5. An employee will accept responsibility if he knows that he will be complimented for a job well done, and not too harshly chastised for failure; that his supervisor will check the cause of the failure, and, if it was the supervisor's fault, he will assume the blame therefore. If it was the employee's fault, his supervisor will explain the correct method or means of handling the responsibility.
6. An employee wants to receive credit for a suggestion he has made, that is used. If a suggestion cannot be used, the employee is entitled to an explanation. The supervisor should not say "no" and close the subject.
7. Fear and worry slow up a worker's ability. Poor working environment can impair his physical and mental health. A good supervisor avoids forceful methods, threats, and arguments to get a job done.
8. A forceful supervisor is able to train his employees individually and as a team, and is able to motivate them in the proper channels.
9. A mature supervisor is able to properly evaluate his subordinates and to keep them happy and satisfied.
10. A sensitive supervisor will never patronize his subordinates.
11. A worthy supervisor will respect his employees' confidences.
12. Definite and clear-cut responsibilities should be assigned to each executive.
13. Responsibility should always be coupled with corresponding authority.
14. No change should be made in the scope or responsibilities of a position without a definite understanding to that effect on the part of all persons concerned.
15. No executive or employee, occupying a single position in the organization, should be subject to definite orders from more than one source.
16. Orders should never be given to subordinates over the head of a responsible executive. Rather than do this, the officer in question should be supplanted.
17. Criticisms of subordinates should, whoever possible, be made privately, and in no case should a subordinate be criticized in the presence of executives or employees of equal or lower rank.
18. No dispute or difference between executives or employees as to authority or responsibilities should be considered too trivial for prompt and careful adjudication.
19. Promotions, wage changes, and disciplinary action should always be approved by the executive immediately superior to the one directly responsible.
20. No executive or employee should ever be required, or expected, to be at the same time an assistant to, and critic of, another.
21. Any executive whose work is subject to regular inspection should, wherever practicable, be given the assistance and facilities necessary to enable him to maintain an independent check of the quality of his work.

MINI-TEXT IN SUPERVISION, ADMINISTRATION, MANAGEMENT, AND ORGANIZATION

I. Brief Highlights

Listed concisely and sequentially are major headings and important data in the field for quick recall and review.

A. Levels of Management

Any organization of some size has several levels of management. In terms of a ladder, the levels are:

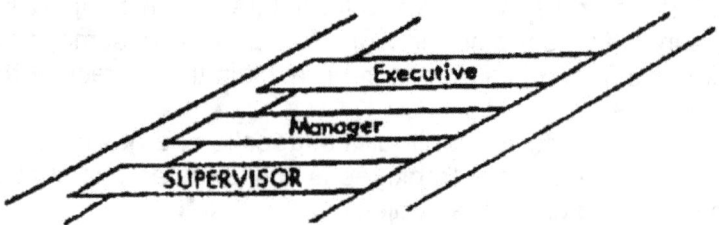

The first level is very important because it is the beginning point of management leadership.

B. What the Supervisor Must Learn

A supervisor must learn to:
1. Deal with people and their differences
2. Get the job done through people
3. Recognize the problems when they exist
4. Overcome obstacles to good performance
5. Evaluate the performance of people
6. Check his own performance in terms of accomplishment

C. A Definition of Supervisor

The term supervisor means any individual having authority, in the interests of the employer, to hire, transfer, suspend, lay-off, recall, promote, discharge, assign, reward, or discipline other employees or responsibility to direct them, or to adjust their grievances, or effectively to recommend such action, if, in connection with the foregoing, exercise of such authority is not of a merely routine or clerical nature but requires the use of independent judgment.

D. Elements of the Team Concept

What is involved in teamwork? The component parts are:
1. Members
2. A leader
3. Goals
4. Plans
5. Cooperation
6. Spirit

E. Principles of Organization
1. A team member must know what his job is.
2. Be sure that the nature and scope of a job are understood.
3. Authority and responsibility should be carefully spelled out.
4. A supervisor should be permitted to make the maximum number of decisions affecting his employees.
5. Employees should report to only one supervisor.
6. A supervisor should direct only as many employees as he can handle effectively.
7. An organization plan should be flexible.

8. Inspection and performance of work should be separate.
9. Organizational problems should receive immediate attention.
10. Assign work in line with ability and experience.

F. The Four Important Parts of Every Job
1. Inherent in every job is the *accountability* for results.
2. A second set of factors in every job is *responsibilities*.
3. Along with duties and responsibilities one must have the *authority* to act within certain limits without obtaining permission to proceed.
4. No job exists in a vacuum. The supervisor is surrounded by key *relationships*.

G. Principles of Delegation
Where work is delegated for the first time, the supervisor should think in terms of these questions:
1. Who is best qualified to do this?
2. Can an employee improve his abilities by doing this?
3. How long should an employee spend on this?
4. Are there any special problems for which he will need guidance?
5. How broad a delegation can I make?

H. Principles of Effective Communications
1. Determine the media.
2. To whom directed?
3. Identification and source authority.
4. Is communication understood?

I. Principles of Work Improvement
1. Most people usually do only the work which is assigned to them.
2. Workers are likely to fit assigned work into the time available to perform it.
3. A good workload usually stimulates output.
4. People usually do their best work when they know that results will be reviewed or inspected.
5. Employees usually feel that someone else is responsible for conditions of work, workplace layout, job methods, type of tools/equipment, and other such factors.
6. Employees are usually defensive about their job security.
7. Employees have natural resistance to change.
8. Employees can support or destroy a supervisor.
9. A supervisor usually earns the respect of his people through his personal example of diligence and efficiency.

J. Areas of Job Improvement
The areas of job improvement are quite numerous, but the most common ones which a supervisor can identify and utilize are:
1. Departmental layout
2. Flow of work
3. Workplace layout
4. Utilization of manpower
5. Work methods
6. Materials handling

7. Utilization
8. Motion economy

K. Seven Key Points in Making Improvements
1. Select the job to be improved
2. Study how it is being done now
3. Question the present method
4. Determine actions to be taken
5. Chart proposed method
6. Get approval and apply
7. Solicit worker participation

I. Corrective Techniques of Job Improvement
Specific Problems
1. Size of workload
2. Inability to meet schedules
3. Strain and fatigue
4. Improper use of men and skills
5. Waste, poor quality, unsafe conditions
6. Bottleneck conditions that hinder output
7. Poor utilization of equipment and machine
8. Efficiency and productivity of labor

General Improvement
1. Departmental layout
2. Flow of work
3. Work plan layout
4. Utilization of manpower
5. Work methods
6. Materials handling
7. Utilization of equipment
8. Motion economy

Corrective Techniques
1. Study with scale model
2. Flow chart study
3. Motion analysis
4. Comparison of units produced to standard allowance
5. Methods analysis
6. Flow chart and equipment study
7. Down time vs. running time
8. Motion analysis

M. A Planning Checklist
1. Objectives
2. Controls
3. Delegations
4. Communications
5. Resources
6. Manpower

7. Equipment
8. Supplies and materials
9. Utilization of time
10. Safety
11. Money
12. Work
13. Timing of improvements

N. Five Characteristics of Good Directions
In order to get results, directions must be:
1. Possible of accomplishment
2. Agreeable with worker interests
3. Related to mission
4. Planned and complete
5. Unmistakably clear

O. Types of Directions
1. Demands or direct orders
2. Requests
3. Suggestion or implication
4. volunteering

P. Controls
A typical listing of the overall areas in which the supervisor should establish controls might be:
1. Manpower
2. Materials
3. Quality of work
4. Quantity of work
5. Time
6. Space
7. Money
8. Methods

Q. Orienting the New Employee
1. Prepare for him
2. Welcome the new employee
3. Orientation for the job
4. Follow-up

R. Checklist for Orienting New Employees   Yes   No
1. Do you appreciate the feelings of new employees
   when they first report for work?   ___   ___
2. Are you aware of the fact that the new employee must
   make a big adjustment to his job?   ___   ___
3. Have you given him good reasons for liking the job and
   the organization?   ___   ___
4. Have you prepared for his first day on the job?   ___   ___
5. Did you welcome him cordially and make him feel needed?   ___   ___

		Yes	No
6.	Did you establish rapport with him so that he feels free to talk and discuss matters with you?	___	___
7.	Did you explain his job to him and his relationship to you?	___	___
8.	Does he know that his work will be evaluated periodically on a basis that is fair and objective?	___	___
9.	Did you introduce him to his fellow workers in such a way that they are likely to accept him?	___	___
10.	Does he know what employee benefits he will receive?	___	___
11.	Does he understand the importance of being on the job and what to do if he must leave his duty station?	___	___
12.	Has he been impressed with the importance of accident prevention and safe practice?	___	___
13.	Does he generally know his way around the department?	___	___
14.	Is he under the guidance of a sponsor who will teach the right way of doing things?	___	___
15.	Do you plan to follow-up so that he will continue to adjust successfully to his job?	___	___

S. Principles of Learning
    1. Motivation
    2. Demonstration or explanation
    3. Practice

T. Causes of Poor Performance
    1. Improper training for job
    2. Wrong tools
    3. Inadequate directions
    4. Lack of supervisory follow-up
    5. Poor communications
    6. Lack of standards of performance
    7. Wrong work habits
    8. Low morale
    9. Other

U. Four Major Steps in On-The-Job Instruction
    1. Prepare the worker
    2. Present the operation
    3. Tryout performance
    4. Follow-up

V. Employees Want Five Things
    1. Security
    2. Opportunity
    3. Recognition
    4. Inclusion
    5. Expression

W. Some Don'ts in Regard to Praise
1. Don't praise a person for something he hasn't done.
2. Don't praise a person unless you can be sincere.
3. Don't be sparing in praise just because your superior withholds it from you.
4. Don't let too much time elapse between good performance and recognition of it

X. How to Gain Your Workers' Confidence
Methods of developing confidence include such things as:
1. Knowing the interests, habits, hobbies of employees
2. Admitting your own inadequacies
3. Sharing and telling of confidence in others
4. Supporting people when they are in trouble
5. Delegating matters that can be well handled
6. Being frank and straightforward about problems and working conditions
7. Encouraging others to bring their problems to you
8. Taking action on problems which impede worker progress

Y. Sources of Employee Problems
On-the-job causes might be such things as:
1. A feeling that favoritism is exercised in assignments
2. Assignment of overtime
3. An undue amount of supervision
4. Changing methods or systems
5. Stealing of ideas or trade secrets
6. Lack of interest in job
7. Threat of reduction in force
8. Ignorance or lack of communications
9. Poor equipment
10. Lack of knowing how supervisor feels toward employee
11. Shift assignments

Off-the-job problems might have to do with:
1. Health
2. Finances
3. Housing
4. Family

Z. The Supervisor's Key to Discipline
There are several key points about discipline which the supervisor should keep in mind:
1. Job discipline is one of the disciplines of life and is directed by the supervisor.
2. It is more important to correct an employee fault than to fix blame for it.
3. Employee performance is affected by problems both on the job and off.
4. Sudden or abrupt changes in behavior can be indications of important employee problems.
5. Problems should be dealt with as soon as possible after they are identified.
6. The attitude of the supervisor may have more to do with solving problems than the techniques of problem solving.
7. Correction of employee behavior should be resorted to only after the supervisor is sure that training or counseling will not be helpful.

8. Be sure to document your disciplinary actions.
9. Make sure that you are disciplining on the basis of facts rather than personal feelings.
10. Take each disciplinary step in order, being careful not to make snap judgments, or decisions based on impatience.

AA. Five Important Processes of Management
1. Planning
2. Organizing
3. Scheduling
4. Controlling
5. Motivating

BB. When the Supervisor Fails to Plan
1. Supervisor creates impression of not knowing his job
2. May lead to excessive overtime
3. Job runs itself—supervisor lacks control
4. Deadlines and appointments missed
5. Parts of the work go undone
6. Work interrupted by emergencies
7. Sets a bad example
8. Uneven workload creates peaks and valleys
9. Too much time on minor details at expense of more important tasks

CC. Fourteen General Principles of Management
1. Division of work
2. Authority and responsibility
3. Discipline
4. Unity of command
5. Unity of direction
6. Subordination of individual interest to general interest
7. Remuneration of personnel
8. Centralization
9. Scalar chain
10. Order
11. Equity
12. Stability of tenure of personnel
13. Initiative
14. Esprit de corps

DD. Change

Bringing about change is perhaps attempted more often, and yet less well understood, than anything else the supervisor does. How do people generally react to change? (People tend to resist change that is imposed upon them by other individuals or circumstances.

Change is characteristic of every situation. It is a part of every real endeavor where the efforts of people are concerned.

13

1. Why do people resist change?
   People may resist change because of:
   a. Fear of the unknown
   b. Implied criticism
   c. Unpleasant experiences in the past
   d. Fear of loss of status
   e. Threat to the ego
   f. Fear of loss of economic stability

2. How can we best overcome the resistance to change?
   In initiating change, take these steps:
   a. Get ready to sell
   b. Identify sources of help
   c. Anticipate objections
   d. Sell benefits
   e. Listen in depth
   f. Follow up

II. Brief Topical Summaries

   A. Who/What is the Supervisor?
   1. The supervisor is often called the "highest level employee and the lowest level manager."
   2. A supervisor is a member of both management and the work group. He acts as a bridge between the two.
   3. Most problems in supervision are in the area of human relations, or people problems.
   4. Employees expect: Respect, opportunity to learn and to advance, and a sense of belonging, and so forth.
   5. Supervisors are responsible for directing people and organizing work. Planning is of paramount importance.
   6. A position description is a set of duties and responsibilities inherent to a given position.
   7. It is important to keep the position description up-to-date and to provide each employee with his own copy.

   B. The Sociology of Work
   1. People are alike in many ways; however, each individual is unique.
   2. The supervisor is challenged in getting to know employee differences. Acquiring skills in evaluating individuals is an asset.
   3. Maintaining meaningful working relationships in the organization is of great importance.
   4. The supervisor has an obligation to help individuals to develop to their fullest potential.
   5. Job rotation on a planned basis helps to build versatility and to maintain interest and enthusiasm in work groups.
   6. Cross training (job rotation) provides backup skills.

7. The supervisor can help reduce tension by maintaining a sense of humor, providing guidance to employees, and by making reasonable and timely decisions. Employees respond favorably to working under reasonably predictable circumstances.
8. Change is characteristic of all managerial behavior. The supervisor must adjust to changes in procedures, new methods, technological changes, and to a number of new and sometimes challenging situations.
9. To overcome the natural tendency for people to resist change, the supervisor should become more skillful in initiating change.

C. Principles and Practices of Supervision
1. Employees should be required to answer to only one superior.
2. A supervisor can effectively direct only a limited number of employees, depending upon the complexity, variety, and proximity of the jobs involved.
3. The organizational chart presents the organization in graphic form. It reflects lines of authority and responsibility as well as interrelationships of units within the organization.
4. Distribution of work can be improved through an analysis using the "Work Distribution Chart."
5. The "Work Distribution Chart" reflects the division of work within a unit in understandable form.
6. When related tasks are given to an employee, he has a better chance of increasing his skills through training.
7. The individual who is given the responsibility for tasks must also be given the appropriate authority to insure adequate results.
8. The supervisor should delegate repetitive, routine work. Preparation of recurring reports, maintaining leave and attendance records are some examples.
9. Good discipline is essential to good task performance. Discipline is reflected in the actions of employees on the job in the absence of supervision.
10. Disciplinary action may have to be taken when the positive aspects of discipline have failed. Reprimand, warning, and suspension are examples of disciplinary action.
11. If a situation calls for a reprimand, be sure it is deserved and remember it is to be done in private.

D. Dynamic Leadership
1. A style is a personal method or manner of exerting influence.
2. Authoritarian leaders often see themselves as the source of power and authority.
3. The democratic leader often perceives the group as the source of authority and power.
4. Supervisors tend to do better when using the pattern of leadership that is most natural for them.
5. Social scientists suggest that the effective supervisor use the leadership style that best fits the problem or circumstances involved.
6. All four styles—telling, selling, consulting, joining—have their place. Using one does not preclude using the other at another time.

7. The theory X point of view assumes that the average person dislikes work, will avoid it whenever possible, and must be coerced to achieve organizational objectives.
8. The theory Y point of view assumes that the average person considers work to be a natural as play, and, when the individual is committed, he requires little supervision or direction to accomplish desired objectives.
9. The leader's basic assumptions concerning human behavior and human nature affect his actions, decisions, and other managerial practices.
10. Dissatisfaction among employees is often present, but difficult to isolate. The supervisor should seek to weaken dissatisfaction by keeping promises, being sincere and considerate, keeping employees informed, and so forth.
11. Constructive suggestions should be encouraged during the natural progress of the work.

E. Processes for Solving Problems
1. People find their daily tasks more meaningful and satisfying when they can improve them.
2. The causes of problems, or the key factors, are often hidden in the background. Ability to solve problems often involves the ability to isolate them from their backgrounds. There is some substance to the cliché that some persons "can't see the forest for the trees."
3. New procedures are often developed from old ones. Problems should be broken down into manageable parts. New ideas can be adapted from old one.
4. People think differently in problem-solving situations. Using a logical, patterned approach is often useful. One approach found to be useful includes these steps:
   a. Define the problem
   b. Establish objectives
   c. Get the facts
   d. Weigh and decide
   e. Take action
   f. Evaluate action

F. Training for Results
1. Participants respond best when they feel training is important to them.
2. The supervisor has responsibility for the training and development of those who report to him.
3. When training is delegated to others, great care must be exercised to insure the trainer has knowledge, aptitude, and interest for his work as a trainer.
4. Training (learning) of some type goes on continually. The most successful supervisor makes certain the learning contributes in a productive manner to operational goals.
5. New employees are particularly susceptible to training. Older employees facing new job situations require specific training, as well as having need for development and growth opportunities.
6. Training needs require continuous monitoring.
7. The training officer of an agency is a professional with a responsibility to assist supervisors in solving training problems.

8. Many of the self-development steps important to the supervisor's own growth are equally important to the development of peers and subordinates. Knowledge of these is important when the supervisor consults with others on development and growth opportunities.

G. Health, Safety, and Accident Prevention
1. Management-minded supervisors take appropriate measures to assist employees in maintaining health and in assuring safe practices in the work environment.
2. Effective safety training and practices help to avoid injury and accidents.
3. Safety should be a management goal. All infractions of safety which are observed should be corrected without exception.
4. Employees' safety attitude, training and instruction, provision of safe tools and equipment, supervision, and leadership are considered highly important factors which contribute to safety and which can be influenced directly by supervisors.
5. When accidents do occur, they should be investigated promptly for very important reasons, including the fact that information which is gained can be used to prevent accidents in the future.

H. Equal Employment Opportunity
1. The supervisor should endeavor to treat all employees fairly, without regard to religion, race, sex, or national origin.
2. Groups tend to reflect the attitude of the leader. Prejudice can be detected even in very subtle form. Supervisors must strive to create a feeling of mutual respect and confidence in every employee.
3. Complete utilization of all human resources is a national goal. Equitable consideration should be accorded women in the work force, minority-group members, the physically and mentally handicapped, and the older employee. The important question is: "Who can do the job?"
4. Training opportunities, recognition for performance, overtime assignments, promotional opportunities, and all other personnel actions are to be handled on an equitable basis.

I. Improving Communications
1. Communications is achieving understanding between the sender and the receiver of a message. It also means sharing information—the creation of understanding.
2. Communication is basic to all human activity. Words are means of conveying meanings; however, real meanings are in people.
3. There are very practical differences in the effectiveness of one-way, impersonal, and two-way communications. Words spoken face-to-face are better understood. Telephone conversations are effective, but lack the rapport of person-to-person exchanges. The whole person communicates.
4. Cooperation and communication in an organization go hand in hand. When there is a mutual respect between people, spelling out rules and procedures for communicating is unnecessary.
5. There are several barriers to effective communications. These include failure to listen with respect and understanding, lack of skill in feedback, and misinterpreting the meanings of words used by the speaker. It is also common

practice to listen to what we want to hear, and tune out things we do not want to hear.
6. Communication is management's chief problem. The supervisor should accept the challenge to communicate more effectively and to improve interagency and intra-agency communications.
7. The supervisor may often plan for and conduct meetings. The planning phase is critical and may determine the success or the failure of a meeting.
8. Speaking before groups usually requires extra effort. Stage fright may never disappear completely, but it can be controlled.

J. Self-Development
1. Every employee is responsible for his own self-development.
2. Toastmaster and toastmistress clubs offer opportunities to improve skills in oral communications.
3. Planning for one's own self-development is of vital importance. Supervisors know their own strengths and limitations better than anyone else.
4. Many opportunities are open to aid the supervisor in his developmental efforts, including job assignments; training opportunities, both governmental and non-governmental—to include universities and professional conferences and seminars.
5. Programmed instruction offers a means of studying at one's own rate.
6. Where difficulties may arise from a supervisor's being away from his work for training, he may participate in televised home study or correspondence courses to meet his self-development needs.

K. Teaching and Training
1. The Teaching Process
Teaching is encouraging and guiding the learning activities of students toward established goals. In most cases this process consists of five steps: preparation, presentation, summarization, evaluation, and application.

   a. Preparation
   Preparation is two-fold in nature; that of the supervisor and the employee. Preparation by the supervisor is absolutely essential to success. He must know what, when, where, how, and whom he will teach. Some of the factors that should be considered are:
   1) The objectives
   2) The materials needed
   3) The methods to be used
   4) Employee participation
   5) Employee interest
   6) Training aids
   7) Evaluation
   8) Summarization

   Employee preparation consists in preparing the employee to receive the material. Probably the most important single factor in the preparation of the employee is arousing and maintaining his interest. He must know the objectives of the training, why he is there, how the material can be used, and its importance to him.

b. Presentation
In presentation, have a carefully designed plan and follow it. The plan should be accurate and complete, yet flexible enough to meet situations as they arise. The method of presentation will be determined by the particular situation and objectives.

c. Summary
A summary should be made at the end of every training unit and program. In addition, there may be internal summaries depending on the nature of the material being taught. The important thing is that the trainee must always be able to understand how each part of the new material relates to the whole.

d. Application
The supervisor must arrange work so the employee will be given a chance to apply new knowledge or skills while the material is still clear in his mind and interest is high. The trainee does not really know whether he has learned the material until he has been given a chance to apply it. If the material is not applied, it loses most of its value.

e. Evaluation
The purpose of all training is to promote learning. To determine whether the training has been a success or failure, the supervisor must evaluate this learning.
In the broadest sense, evaluation includes all the devices, methods, skills, and techniques used by the supervisor to keep himself and the employees informed as to their progress toward the objectives they are pursuing. The extent to which the employee has mastered the knowledge, skills, and abilities, or changed his attitudes, as determined by the program objectives, is the extent to which instruction has succeeded or failed.
Evaluation should not be confined to the end of the lesson, day, or program but should be used continuously. We shall note later the way this relates to the rest of the teaching process.

2. Teaching Methods
A teaching method is a pattern of identifiable student and instructor activity used in presenting training material.
All supervisors are faced with the problem of deciding which method should be used at a given time.

a. Lecture
The lecture is direct oral presentation of material by the supervisor. The present trend is to place less emphasis on the trainer's activity and more on that of the trainee.

b. Discussion
Teaching by discussion or conference involves using questions and other techniques to arouse interest and focus attention upon certain areas, and by doing so creating a learning situation. This can be one of the most

valuable methods because it gives the employees an opportunity to express their ideas and pool their knowledge.

    c. Demonstration
The demonstration is used to teach how something works or how to do something. It can be used to show a principle or what the results of a series of actions will be. A well-staged demonstration is particularly effective because it shows proper methods of performance in a realistic manner.

    d. Performance
Performance is one of the most fundamental of all learning techniques or teaching methods. The trainee may be able to tell how a specific operation should be performed but he cannot be sure he knows how to perform the operation until he has done so.
As with all methods, there are certain advantages and disadvantages to each method.

    e. Which Method to Use
Moreover, there are other methods and techniques of teaching. It is difficult to use any method without other methods entering into it. In any learning situation, a combination of methods is usually more effective than any one method alone.

Finally, evaluation must be integrated into the other aspects of the teaching-learning process.

It must be used in the motivation of the trainees; it must be used to assist in developing understanding during the training; and it must be related to employee application of the results of training.

This is distinctly the role of the supervisor.

———

www.ingramcontent.com/pod-product-compliance
Lightning Source LLC
Chambersburg PA
CBHW080323020526

44117CB00035B/2615